KEN·HOM'S VEGETABLE& PASTA·BOOK

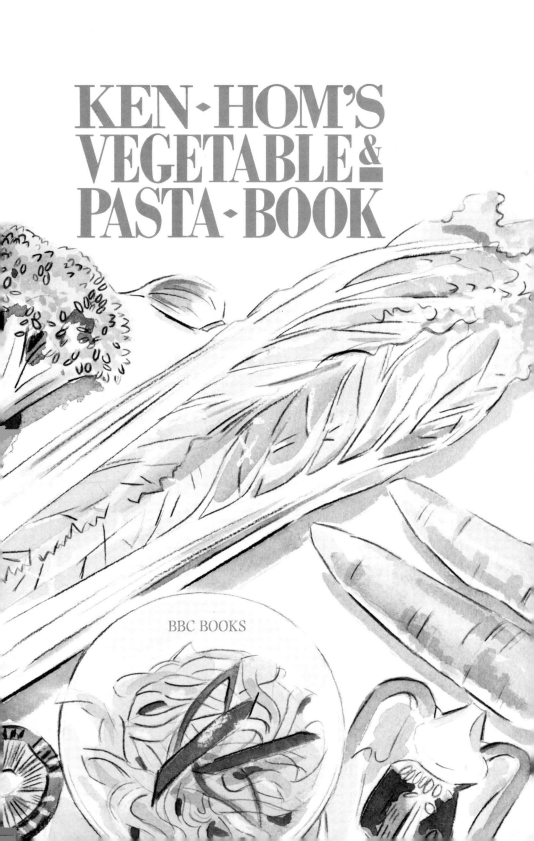

KEN·HOM'S VEGETABLE & PASTA·BOOK

BBC BOOKS

To Madhur Jaffrey
A superb cook and good friend,
your natural elegance is an inspiration.

Cover photograph: Victor Budnik
Food photography: James Jackson
Food prepared for photography: Allyson Birch
Stylist: Jacky Jackson
Illustrations: Angela Barnes
Technical illustrations: Will Giles

Published by BBC Books,
A division of BBC Enterprises Ltd,
Woodlands, 80 Wood Lane,
London W12 0TT

First published 1987
Reprinted 1987

© Taurom Inc/Ken Hom 1987

ISBN 0 563 20540 7 (paperback)
ISBN 0 563 20539 3 (hardback)

Typeset in 11/13 pt Photina and bound in
Great Britain by Butler & Tanner Ltd
Colour printed by Chorley and Pickersgill Ltd

CONTENTS

Acknowledgements 6

Introduction 7

Conversion Table 10

Ingredients 11

Equipment 27

Techniques 31

1 Starters and Appetisers 37

2 Soups 55

3 Cold Dishes and Salads 71

4 Vegetable Dishes 83

5 Beancurd Dishes 115

6 Hot Pasta and Noodles 129

7 Cold Pasta and Noodles 149

8 Rice 159

9 Desserts 173

10 Suggested Menus 181

Mail-Order Suppliers 187

Index 189

ACKNOWLEDGEMENTS

A cookery book requires meticulous attention to detail and it is almost impossible for the author, without the help of others, to do everything that must be done to make it as useful and interesting as possible. This book is no exception. I owe an immense debt to Gordon Wing, who is a great chef in his own right. His unerring good taste and expert working and testing of the recipes helped ensure their accuracy. I am grateful to Mimi Luebbermann for her considerable editorial skills and talents of organisation. Her vast experience and many useful suggestions helped make this a better book. My thanks and appreciation go to Gerry Cavanaugh, whose skilful research and editing helped me to clarify my thoughts and to present them precisely.

I feel fortunate to be associated with BBC Books and to have Nina Shandloff as my editor there. I am grateful to them for their generous encouragement.

Credit should go also to Gillian Shaw for the design of the book and to James Jackson for the photography.

And for playing no small part in this book and all of my professional activities, my thanks to Ted Lyman, my agent for my international affairs, and Martha Casselman, my American literary agent. Their sound advice and good sense have been of incalculable benefit to me over the years and they have my deep appreciation.

INTRODUCTION

One of the most exciting culinary developments in recent years has been the introduction into Western cuisine of a whole range of Chinese, Japanese and Southeast Asian methods and ingredients, especially the seasonings. Flavours that used to be 'exotic' – chilli oil, coconut milk, lemongrass, bean thread (transparent) noodles, rice wine, star anise, Sichuan peppercorns, soy sauce, fresh ginger and fresh coriander – are now well on their way to becoming standards in home cooking. Most of the recipes in this book are drawn from the Chinese tradition, which is the basis of my own style, and much of the information given in the introductory sections will be familiar to readers of my earlier book on Chinese cookery. However, here I have also included a representative sampling of dishes from other Eastern cuisines.

Each recipe reflects my own tastes and preferences and is drawn from my own observations and experiences – on my travels in Southeast Asia, in restaurants and conversations with other chefs, in my reading and in my culinary experiments. The result is a very personal, eclectic collection which nevertheless has a unified theme: good food, especially vegetables and pasta, that is delicious, flavourful and easily prepared, with an oriental flair that blends congenially with a Western meal.

Growing up within the Chinese culinary tradition, fresh vegetables, noodles and pasta – wonderful foods – have been central to my diet in both my personal and professional life ever since I can remember. I use the Italian word 'pasta' because it has entered our vocabulary – covering various forms of unleavened dough, extruded, rolled out, sliced and moulded into different forms. When I was a child, Chinese pasta (of which there are many types, shapes and sizes) and vegetables were as much a part of my diet as were rice and beancurd. As a professional chef, food writer and cookery author, I have always emphasised the role of vegetables and pasta in any cookery. This is especially true as I have become more and more aware of the variety of pastas outside my Chinese influence.

When I became old enough to venture out into the mainstream of Western culture, I was appalled by the way vegetables and pasta were cooked. I had always loved vegetables but I understood my schoolmates' aversion to them, overcooked as they were to the point of limpness and tastelessness. As for pasta, it was gummy and devoid of its customary textures and subtle tastes, overcooked and drowned in tomato sauce. I thought it all quite unnecessary.

In the Chinese cultural environment, food is a source of happiness for both body and soul; meal times are times of an almost religious sharing, of conversation and family interaction, with proper attention having been paid to the preparation of the foods. My mother prepared meat, fish and poultry dishes, but they never dominated our table. Rather, vegetables and pasta, with rice too of course, were the mainstay of our diet. Vegetables, both Chinese and European varieties, were more important to us than meats. And I relished them, finding them flavourful, colourful and cooked to perfection. This means, among other things, that vegetables were preferably as fresh as possible and never overcooked – preserving their natural flavours and nutrients. So too were our noodle and pasta dishes, prepared so that they retained their textures and tastes and were never overwhelmed by any sauce. Pasta, usually in the form of noodles, was enjoyed either as a snack or quick meal, or as an integral part of the complete meal. I savoured them in many forms: fresh or dried egg noodles, flour noodles, rice noodles, wuntuns and spring rolls. Today, of course, I include in my everyday diet the wonderful varieties of European pasta, combined with a blending of oriental seasonings, spices and stuffings.

I agree with a food critic who wrote that the phrase 'al dente' is both overworked and vague; the only workable test of doneness for both vegetables and pasta is the 'nibble test'. Be prepared to nibble or taste your foods during preparation, as only you can tell when they are ready.

I must emphasise that this is *not* a vegetarian cookbook, although it can be used very usefully by vegetarians. I am not a vegetarian myself; my own diet consists primarily of vegetables, rice, pasta or noodles and seafood, with poultry and meat quite secondary and always in small portions. Many of the recipes in this book can accompany other dishes, oriental or not, vegetarian or not, for lunch, dinner or supper. As such, the recipes embody the ideas, tastes, flavours, colours, aromas and aesthetics inspired by my own dual Asian–Western tradition. You may, if you wish, add meat or poultry to some of the recipes – whatever your own taste tells you is appropriate. The recipes are basically authentic but reflect my own tastes and experiences; use them and experiment to make them your own. I can only be a guide on your first steps into this delightful terrain. Your taste and imagination, with loving care in your preparations, will take you much further than any guide could ever do. Happy cooking and eating!

Conversion Table

All these are approximate conversions, which have either been rounded up or down. In a few recipes it has been necessary to modify them very slightly. Never mix metric and imperial measures in one recipe. Stick to one system or the other.

Weights	
$\frac{1}{2}$ oz	10 g
1	25
$1\frac{1}{2}$	40
2	50
3	75
4	110
5	150
6	175
7	200
8	225
9	250
10	275
12	350
13	375
14	400
15	425
1 lb	450
$1\frac{1}{4}$	550
$1\frac{1}{2}$	700
2	900
3	1.4 kg
4	1.8
5	2.3

Volume	
1 fl oz	25 ml
2	50
3	75
5 ($\frac{1}{4}$ pint)	150
10 ($\frac{1}{2}$)	300
15 ($\frac{3}{4}$)	400
1 pint	570
$1\frac{1}{4}$	700
$1\frac{1}{2}$	900
$1\frac{3}{4}$	1 litre
2	1.1
$2\frac{1}{4}$	1.3
$2\frac{1}{2}$	1.4
$2\frac{3}{4}$	1.6
3	1.7
$3\frac{1}{4}$	1.8
$3\frac{1}{2}$	2
$3\frac{3}{4}$	2.1
4	2.3
5	2.8
6	3.4
7	4.0
8 (1 gal)	4.5

Measurements	
$\frac{1}{4}$ inch	0.5 cm
$\frac{1}{2}$	1
1	2.5
2	5
3	7.5
4	10
6	15
7	18
8	20.5
9	23
11	28
12	30.5

Oven temperatures		
Mk 1	275°F	140°C
2	300	150
3	325	170
4	350	180
5	375	190
6	400	200
7	425	220
8	450	230
9	475	240

Ingredients

Fresh vegetables are, of course, essential to good cooking. But equally important are the other ingredients – the seasonings, spices and sauces that complement and enhance the virtues of the vegetables. The recipes in this book draw upon a number of special ingredients which give a distinctive taste to the vegetables and pasta, making them authentic versions of the Chinese, Japanese and Southeast Asian originals.

All the ingredients used in these recipes can be obtained in this country, if not from your local supermarket than certainly from either a Chinese, oriental or Asian grocer. There are now many of these grocers throughout the UK and a list is given at the back of this book (page 187) of some who offer a mail-order service. It is well worth the effort to find your nearest oriental, Chinese or Asian grocer and to build up a stock of the most frequently used ingredients.

One ingredient commonly used, which you will *not* find mentioned here, is the additive monosodium glutamate (also known as MSG, Ve Tsin, Accent, seasoning or taste powder). This is a white crystalline extract of grains and vegetables widely used to tenderise and enhance the natural flavour of certain foods. Some people experience an adverse reaction to it, suffering symptoms such as headaches, excessive thirst and heart palpitations. This allergic response is sometimes known as 'Chinese restaurant syndrome'. I believe that the freshest and finest ingredients need no enhancing and therefore I never use monosodium glutamate.

Below I have listed, in alphabetical order, all the special ingredients used in the book. More detailed information on specific vegetables and types of pasta and noodles is given in the introductions to those chapters.

BAMBOO SHOOTS

Bamboo shoots are the young edible shoots of certain kinds of bamboo. In this country, they are only available tinned. Pale yellow with a crunchy texture, they come peeled and either whole or thickly sliced. They can be bought in most supermarkets, delicatessens and in Chinese grocers. Rinse them thoroughly before use and transfer any remaining shoots to a jar, cover them with fresh water and keep in the refrigerator. If the water is changed daily they will keep for up to a week.

BEANCURD

Beancurd is also known by its Chinese name, 'doufu', or by its Japanese name, 'tofu'. It has played an important part in Chinese cookery for over 1000 years: it is highly nutritious, being rich in protein, and combines well with other foods. Beancurd has a distinctive texture but a bland taste. It is made from yellow soya beans which are soaked, ground, mixed with water and then cooked briefly before being solidified. In this country, it is usually sold in two forms, firm cakes or as a thickish junket, but it is also available in several dried forms and fermented. The soft junket-like variety (sometimes called silken tofu) is used for soups and other dishes, while the solid type is used for stir-frying, braising and poaching. Solid beancurd 'cakes' are white in colour and are sold in Chinese grocers and in many health food shops. They are packed in water in plastic containers and may be kept in this state in the refrigerator for up to 5 days, providing the water is changed daily. To use solid beancurd, cut the amount required into cubes or shreds using a sharp knife. Do this with care as it is delicate. Beancurd also needs to be cooked carefully as too much stirring can cause it to disintegrate.

Fermented beancurd

A cheese-like form of beancurd preserved in rice wine, brine with rice or chillies, and sold in glass jars in Chinese grocers. It is used as a flavouring agent, especially for vegetables. A little can add zest to any vegetable dish. Once it begins to cook, it produces a fragrant odour that enriches vegetables. Fermented beancurd comes in several forms: the red fermented beancurd has been cured in a brine with red rice, the chilli one has flecks of crushed chilli peppers and the ordinary one is left plain. Once the jar is opened, it should be stored in the refrigerator, keeping well for several months. There is no substitute for this unique ingredient.

Pressed seasoned beancurd

When water is extracted from fresh beancurd cakes by pressing them with a weight, the beancurd becomes firm and compact. Simmered in water with soy sauce, star anise and sugar, the pressed beancurd acquires a brownish colour and smooth, resilient texture. Cut into small pieces, it can be stir-fried with meat or vegetables; and when cut into larger pieces, it can be simmered. In China, pressed beancurd is a popular offering at many food stalls. It can be found in Chinese grocers. Substitute fresh firm beancurd if it is unavailable.

BLACK BEANS

These small black soya beans, also known as salted black beans, are preserved by being fermented with salt and spices. They have a distinctive, slightly salty taste and a pleasantly rich smell, and are used as a seasoning, often in conjunction with garlic and fresh ginger. Black beans are inexpensive and can be obtained from Chinese grocers, usually in tins, as 'black beans in salted sauce'; you may also see them packed in plastic bags, which are preferable. Rinse before use; I prefer to chop the beans slightly too. Transfer any unused beans and liquid to a sealed jar and they will keep indefinitely if stored in the refrigerator.

CHILLIES

Chillies are used extensively in western China and somewhat less frequently in the south, as well as many parts of Southeast Asia. They are the seed pods of the capsicum plant and can be obtained fresh, dried or ground.

Fresh chillies

Fresh chillies can be distinguished by their small size and elongated shape. They should look fresh and bright with no brown patches or black spots. There are several varieties. Red chillies are generally milder than green ones because they sweeten as they ripen.

To prepare fresh chillies, first rinse them in cold water. Using a small sharp knife, slit them lengthways and remove and discard the seeds. Rinse the chillies well under cold running water, and then prepare them according to the instructions in the recipe. Wash your hands, knife and chopping board before preparing other foods, and be careful not to touch your eyes until you have washed your hands thoroughly with soap and water.

Dried red chillies

Dried red chillies are small and thin, and about $\frac{1}{2}$ inch (1 cm) long. They are used to season oil for stir-fried dishes, sauces and for braising. Dried chillies are normally left whole or cut in half lengthways and the seeds left in. The Chinese like them to blacken and remain in the dish during cooking, but as they are extremely hot and spicy, you may choose to remove them after using them to flavour the cooking oil. Dried chillies can be found in most supermarkets and in Chinese and oriental grocers, and will keep indefinitely in a tightly covered jar.

Chilli powder

Chilli powder, also known as cayenne pepper, is made from ground dried red chillies. It is pungent, aromatic and ranges from hot to very hot; it is therefore widely used in many spicy dishes. You will be able to buy chilli powder in any supermarket.

Chilli bean sauce (see SAUCES AND PASTES)
Chilli oil (see OILS)
Chilli sauce (see SAUCES AND PASTES)

CINNAMON STICKS/BARK

Cinnamon sticks are curled, paper-thin pieces of the bark of the cinnamon tree. Chinese cinnamon comes as thicker sticks of this bark. It is highly aromatic and more pungent than the more common cinnamon sticks, but the latter are an adequate substitute. They add a robust taste to braised dishes and are an important ingredient of five spice powder. Store cinnamon sticks or bark in a tightly sealed jar to preserve their aroma and flavour. Ground cinnamon is not a satisfactory substitute.

COCONUT MILK

You can make your own coconut milk according to this recipe:

1 small coconut
1¼ pints (700 ml) low-fat milk
6 tablespoons sugar

Pre-heat the oven to gas mark 4, 350°F (180°C). To prepare the coconut, pierce two of the 'eyes' in the shell and drain and discard the liquid inside. Place the drained coconut in the oven for about 20 minutes. If this does not crack the shell, split it by tapping with a hammer along its line of cleavage until the coconut breaks apart. (Wrap the coconut in a towel while cracking it to prevent the small pieces from flying about.) Remove the white meat with a knife, discarding any of the brown skin.

Cut the coconut into small pieces and place in a medium-sized saucepan. Cover with 17 fl oz (450 ml) of the milk and simmer for 10 minutes. Allow to cool, then process in a blender on high speed for 1 minute. Let the coconut stand for 15 minutes, then strain into a bowl. Using the back of a wooden spoon, squeeze all the liquid from the chopped coconut. Return the coconut milk to the pan, add the sugar and remaining milk. Simmer for 5 minutes until the milk thickens. Allow to cool, then refrigerate.

Alternatively you can use the tinned variety. I have found the tinned version quite acceptable and a lot less work. Look for the ones from Thailand or Malaysia. You can find them in Chinese or oriental grocers, usually in 14 fl oz (375 ml) or 15 fl oz (400 ml) tins. Shake the tins well before opening to use. If you are using tinned milk, any remainder can be kept in the refrigerator for at least a week out of the tin.

CORIANDER (CHINESE PARSLEY)

Fresh coriander is one of the relatively few herbs used in Chinese cookery. It looks like flat parsley but its pungent, musky, citrus-like flavour gives it a distinctive and unmistakeable character. Its feathery leaves are often used as a garnish or it can be chopped and then mixed into sauces and stuffings. Parsley may be used as a substitute but, for an authentic Chinese flavour, it is well worth trying to obtain the real thing. Many Chinese, oriental and Asian grocers stock fresh coriander, as do some greengrocers and super-markets now. When buying fresh coriander, look for deep green, fresh-looking leaves. Yellow and limp leaves indicate age and should be avoided.

To store coriander, wash in cold water, drain thoroughly and put it in a clean polythene bag with a couple of sheets of moist kitchen paper. Stored in the vegetable compartment of the refriger-ator, it should keep for several days.

CORNFLOUR

In China and Southeast Asia there are many flours and types of starch, such as waterchestnut powder, taro starch and arrowroot, which are used to bind and thicken sauces and to make batter. These exotic starches and flours are difficult to obtain but I have found cornflour works just as well in my recipes. As part of a marinade, it helps to coat the food properly and gives dishes a velvety texture. Cornflour also protects food during deep-frying by helping to seal in the juices, and it can also be used as a binder for minced stuffings. Cornflour is invariably blended with cold water until it forms a smooth paste before it is used in sauces.

DASHI

Dashi is a clear stock made from dried bonito (tuna) flakes and seaweed. This is the basis for most Japanese soups. You can make dashi by purchasing the dried bonita flakes and simmering it in water, or you can purchase instant dashi from shops selling Japanese food products. Simply follow the instructions on the packet. I have found the instant dashi quite acceptable. Make up only enough to use at the time.

FIVE SPICE POWDER

Five spice powder is less commonly known as five-flavoured powder or five fragrance spice powder, and is available in many super-markets (in the spice section) and in Chinese grocers. This brownish powder is a mixture of star anise, Sichuan peppercorns, fennel, cloves and cinnamon. A good blend is pungent, fragrant, spicy and slightly sweet at the same time. The exotic fragrance it gives to a dish makes the search for a good mixture well worth the effort. It keeps indefinitely in a well sealed jar.

FLOURS
Glutinous rice flour
This flour is made from glutinous rice and is often used in making pastries to give the chewy texture to the doughs. Available from Chinese grocers, this is not an acceptable substitute for rice flour.
Rice flour
This flour is made from raw rice and is used to make fresh rice noodles. Obtainable from Chinese grocers, it is stored as plain flour.

FUNGUS (see MUSHROOMS, CHINESE DRIED)

GARLIC

Garlic has been an essential seasoning in oriental cookery for thousands of years. It would be inconceivable to cook without the distinctive, highly aromatic smell and taste of garlic. Throughout Asia it is used in numerous ways: whole, finely chopped, crushed and pickled. It is used to flavour oils as well as spicy sauces, and is often paired with other equally pungent ingredients such as spring onions, black beans, curry, fish sauce or fresh ginger.

Select fresh garlic which is firm and preferably pinkish in colour. It should be stored in a cool, dry place but not in the refrigerator where it can easily become mildewed or begin sprouting.

GINGER

Fresh root ginger (actually a rhizome, not a root) is indispensable in oriental cookery. Its pungent, spicy and fresh taste adds a subtle but distinctive flavour to soups, meats, fish, sauces and vegetables. Fresh ginger looks rather like a gnarled Jerusalem artichoke and can range in size from 3 inches (7.5 cm) to 6 inches (15 cm) long. It has pale brown, dry skin which is usually peeled away before use. Select fresh ginger which is firm with no signs of shrivelling. It will keep in the refrigerator, well wrapped in clingfilm, for up to 2 weeks. Fresh ginger can now be found at many greengrocers and supermarkets, and in most Chinese and oriental grocers. Dried powdered ginger has a quite different flavour and cannot be substituted for fresh ginger.

Ginger juice

Ginger juice is made from fresh ginger and is used in cooking to give a subtle ginger taste without the bite of the chopped fresh pieces. To make ginger juice, simply take a piece of fresh ginger and smash it with a kitchen mallet or the side of a cleaver or knife until most of the fibres are exposed. Then, with a garlic press or your hands, simply squeeze out the juice. The left-over ginger can be used to flavour the oil before you cook. The fresh ginger juice must be used immediately.

LEMONGRASS

This aromatic lemony tropical grass is widely used in Southeast Asian cooking and is found in Chinese and oriental grocers. Look for pale green tops and make sure the lemongrass is not dried out. Cut off the fibrous base and peel away the outside layers. Cut off the tops and save to flavour oils or soups. Lemon juice or lemon zest can be used as a substitute. Lemongrass can be sliced and frozen for future use.

LILY BUDS

Also known as tiger lily buds, golden needles or lily stems, dried lily buds (*Lilium Lancifolium*) are an ingredient in Mu Shu dishes and hot and sour soups. They add more texture than taste. Soak the buds in hot water for about 30 minutes or until soft. Cut off the hard ends and shred or cut in half according to the recipe.

MUSHROOMS, CHINESE DRIED

There are many varieties of these which add a particular flavour and aroma to Chinese dishes. These mushrooms can be black or brown in colour. The very large ones, with a lighter colour and a highly cracked surface, are the best and so they are usually the most expensive. They can be bought in boxes or plastic bags from Chinese grocers, and are fairly pricey. Keep them stored in an airtight jar in a cool dry place.

To use Chinese dried mushrooms
Soak the required amount in hot water for about 20 minutes until soft. Squeeze out any excess liquid and remove the tough, inedible stalk. The mushrooms are now ready for use. The resulting liquid can be used for cooking rice – simply pour off the liquid gently, leaving any sand or residue behind.

Chinese dried cloud ears (black fungus)
These tiny dried mushrooms are known as cloud ears because when soaked, they look like little clouds. Soak the cloud ears in hot water for 20–30 minutes until soft. Rinse well and cut away any hard pieces. They are valued for their crunchy texture and slightly smokey flavour. There is some medical research that indicates they are of value in the prevention of heart disease. You can find cloud ears in Chinese or oriental grocers, usually wrapped in plastic or cellophane bags. They keep indefinitely in a jar stored in a cool dry place.

Chinese dried wood ears
These mushrooms are the larger variety of cloud ears. Prepare and soak them in the same way, then rinse well. Once soaked, they will swell up to four or five times their size. Cut away any hard pieces. Sold in Chinese or oriental grocers, they keep indefinitely when stored in a cool dry place.

NORI (see **SEAWEED**)

OILS
Oil is the most commonly used cooking medium in China, Japan and Southeast Asia. The favourite is groundnut (peanut) oil. Animal fats, usually lard and chicken fat, are also used in some areas, particularly in Indonesia and parts of China. I always prefer to use oil since I find animal fats too heavy.

I find oils are best re-used just once or twice, this is healthier since constantly re-using oils increases the saturated fat content. To prepare oil for re-use, simply cool the oil after use and filter it through muslin or a fine strainer into a jar. Cover tightly and keep in a cool, dry place. If you keep oil in the refrigerator it will become cloudy, but it clarifies again at room temperature.

Groundnut oil

This is also known as peanut oil or arachide oil. I prefer to use this because it has a pleasant, mild taste which is unobtrusive. Although it has a higher saturated fat content than some oils, its ability to be heated to a high temperature makes it perfect for stir-frying and deep-frying. Many supermarkets stock groundnut oil, but if you cannot find it use corn oil instead.

Corn oil

Corn or maize oil is also quite suitable for cooking. It has a high heating point although I find it rather bland, plus it has a slightly disagreeable smell. Corn oil is high in polyunsaturates and is therefore one of the healthier oils.

Other vegetable oils

Some of the cheaper vegetable oils available include soyabean, safflower and sunflower oils. They are light in colour and taste, and can also be used in cooking.

Sesame oil

This is a thick, rich, golden brown oil made from sesame seeds, which has a distinctive, nutty flavour and aroma. It is widely used in Chinese and Japanese cookery as a seasoning, but is not normally used as a cooking oil because it heats rapidly and burns easily. It is often added at the last moment to finish a dish. It is sold in bottles in many supermarkets and in Chinese or oriental grocers.

Chilli oil

Chilli oil is an essential ingredient in many of the recipes in this book. This is to be expected, inasmuch as it is a staple condiment/flavouring throughout Asia. You may purchase it in Chinese, oriental or Asian grocers and specialist food shops. The Thai and Malaysian versions are especially hot; the Hong Kong, Taiwanese and Chinese versions are a little milder. Such commercial products are quite acceptable and I include this recipe only because the home-made version is the best. Remember that chilli oil is too dramatic to be used directly in cooking; it is best applied as a final spicy touch. I include the spices (pepper and black beans) for additional flavours, because then it can also be used as a dipping sauce. If you prefer a milder taste, you can reduce the quantity of chopped dried chillies.

Once made, the chilli oil can be put in a tightly sealed glass jar and stored in a cool dark place where it will keep for months.

CHILLI OIL/DIPPING SAUCE

5 fl oz (150 ml) oil, preferably groundnut
2 tablespoons chopped dried red chillies
1 tablespoon unroasted whole Sichuan peppercorns
2 tablespoons whole black beans

Heat a frying-pan or wok over a high heat and add the oil. Put in the rest of the ingredients and cook over a low heat for about 10 minutes. Allow the mixture to cool undisturbed and then pour it into a jar. Leave the mixture to stand for 2 days. Strain and discard the solids from the chilli oil, returning the oil to the glass jar for use in recipes. It will keep indefinitely.

PEANUTS

Raw peanuts are used in oriental cooking to add flavour and a crunchy texture, and are especially popular in Southeast Asian cooking. They can be bought in health food shops, good super-markets and Chinese grocers. The thin red skins need to be removed before you use the nuts. To do this, simply immerse them in a pan of boiling water for about 2 minutes. Drain them, leave to cool and the skins will come off easily.

RED IN SNOW

This is Chinese pickled cabbage that can be bought in tins in Chinese grocers. It adds a pungent slightly sour taste to dishes when used as a flavouring, or it can be used as an interestingly textured vegetable in stir-fried dishes.

RICE WINE

This wine is used extensively for cooking and drinking throughout China and the finest variety is believed to be that from Shaoxing in Zhejiang Province in eastern China. It is made from glutinous rice, yeast and spring water. Available from Chinese grocers, it should be kept at room temperature, tightly corked. A good quality, dry pale sherry can be substituted but cannot equal the rich, mellow taste of Chinese rice wine. Do not confuse this with sake, which is the Japanese version of rice wine and quite different. Rice wine can be found in Chinese grocers.

SAKE

Sake is a Japanese rice wine often used in Japanese cooking.

It should not be confused with Mirin which is a much sweeter wine and cannot be used as a substitute. The more expensive brands are served gently warmed as a drink, but less expensive brands are suitable for cooking. If you do not like the alcohol taste, briefly bring the sake to the boil before combining with other ingredients.

SAUCES AND PASTES

Chinese, Japanese and Southeast Asian cookery involves a number of thick tasty sauces or pastes. They are essential to the authentic taste of the food and it is well worth making the effort to obtain them. Most are sold in bottles or tins in Chinese or oriental grocers and some supermarkets. Tinned sauces, once opened, should be transferred to screw-top glass jars and kept in the refrigerator, where they will last for a long time.

Chilli bean sauce

This is a thick dark sauce or paste made from soya beans, chillies and other seasonings, and is very hot and spicy. Widely used in cooking in western China, it is usually available here in jars in Chinese grocers. Be sure to seal the jar tightly after use and store in the larder or refrigerator. Do not confuse it with chilli sauce (see below) which is a hot, red, thinner sauce made without beans and used mainly as a dipping sauce for cooked dishes. There are Southeast Asian versions of chilli bean sauce and I find them very spicy and hot. You can use these if you like, but throughout this book, I have used the Chinese chilli bean sauce which is slightly milder.

Chilli sauce

Chilli sauce is a hot, bright red sauce made from chillies, vinegar, sugar and salt. It is sometimes used for cooking, but is mainly used as a dipping sauce. There are various brands available in many supermarkets and Chinese grocers and you should experiment with them until you find the one you like best. If you find it too strong, dilute with hot water. Do not confuse this sauce with the chilli bean sauce mentioned previously, which is a much thicker, darker sauce used for cooking.

Curry paste

This prepared paste has a stronger curry flavour than the powdered variety. The spices are mixed with oil and chilli peppers. Be sure to get the Indian variety which is generally the best. You can find curry paste in Asian or Chinese grocers. Kept refrigerated after opening, curry paste keeps indefinitely.

Dipping sauces and mixtures

Many Chinese and Southeast Asian dishes and snacks are dipped
into a variety of dipping sauces before being eaten. The most
popular of these are chilli sauce and chilli oil (see Oils). Soy sauces
and red and black Chinese rice vinegars (see Vinegars) are also
widely used as dips. Some recipes for dipping sauces accompany
particular dishes, but they can easily be served with others.

Fish sauce

Fish sauce, also known as fish gravy or 'nam pla', is a thin brownish
sauce made from fermented salted fresh fish. It is sold bottled and
has a very fish odour and salty taste. Cooking greatly diminishes
the 'fishy' flavour and the sauce adds a subtle taste to many dishes.
You can find it in Chinese or oriental grocers.

Hoisin sauce

This is a thick, dark, brownish red sauce, made from soya beans,
vinegar, sugar, spices and other flavourings. It is sweet and spicy
and is widely used in southern Chinese cookery. In the West, it is
often used as a sauce for Peking Duck instead of the traditional
sweet bean sauce. Hoisin sauce, sometimes called barbecue sauce,
is sold in tins and jars, and is available in Chinese grocers and
some supermarkets. If refrigerated, it should keep indefinitely.

Oyster sauce

This thick brown sauce is made from a concentrate of oysters
cooked in soy sauce and brine. Despite its name, oyster sauce does
not taste fishy. It has a rich flavour and is used not only in cooking
but also as a condiment, diluted with a little oil, for vegetables,
poultry or meats. Oyster sauce is usually sold in bottles and can be
bought in Chinese grocers and some supermarkets. I find it keeps
best in the refrigerator.

Sesame paste

This rich, thick, creamy brown paste is made from sesame seeds.
It is used in both hot and cold dishes, and is particularly popular
in northern and western China. Sesame paste is sold in jars in
Chinese grocers. If you cannot obtain it, use peanut butter.

SOY SAUCES

Soy sauce is an essential ingredient in Chinese and Southeast Asian
cooking. It is made from a mixture of soya beans, flour and water,
which is then naturally fermented and matured for some months.
The liquid which is finally distilled is soy sauce. There are two
main types, light and dark.

Light soy sauce

As the name implies, this is light in colour but it is full of flavour and is the best one to use for cooking. It is saltier than dark soy sauce. In Chinese grocers, light soy sauce is known as Superior Soy.

Dark soy sauce

This sauce is matured for much longer than light soy sauce, hence its darker, almost black, colour. Slightly thicker and stronger than light soy sauce, it is more suitable for stews. I prefer it to light soy sauce as a dipping sauce. It is known in Chinese grocers as Soy Superior Sauce.

Most soy sauces sold in supermarkets are dark soy. Chinese grocers sell both types and the quality is superior. Be sure you buy the right one as the names are very similar.

Yellow bean sauce

This thick, spicy, aromatic sauce is made with yellow beans, flour and salt which are fermented together. It is quite salty but adds a distinctive flavour to Chinese sauces. There are two forms: whole beans in a thick sauce or mashed or puréed beans (sold as crushed yellow bean sauce). I prefer the whole bean variety because it is slightly less salty and has a better texture. It keeps best in the refrigerator.

SEAWEED

Known as nori, seaweed is a nutritious and ancient food. Often used in soups and as a wrapper for sushi, it has a delicate flavour. Nori comes packaged in ten or more thinly pressed dried sheets. Individual recipes use different techniques for soaking and cooking seaweed.

SESAME SEEDS

These are dried seeds of an oriental annual herb. Unhulled, the seeds range from greyish white to black in colour, but once the hull is removed, the sesame seeds are flat, tiny, creamy coloured, and pointed at one end. Sesame seeds are valued as a flavouring agent and as a source of oil and paste. Sesame seeds can be found in supermarkets or Chinese grocers. Kept in a glass jar in a cool dry place, they will last indefinitely.

To toast sesame seeds

Preheat the oven to gas mark 3, 325°F (170°C). Spread the sesame seeds on a baking tray. Roast in the oven for about 10–15 minutes until they are lightly browned. Allow the toasted seeds to cool, then store them in a glass jar.

SHERRY
If you cannot obtain rice wine, you can use a good quality, dry, pale sherry instead. Do not use sweet or cream sherries.

SHRIMPS, DRIED
Dried shrimps are sold in packets in Chinese grocers. Look for the brands with the pinkest colour and avoid greyish coloured ones. They will keep indefinitely stored in a cool dry place. When cooked, dried shrimps add a delicate taste to sauces, unlike the way they smell when purchased. The shrimps are sometimes ground to a paste.

SICHUAN PEPPERCORNS
Sichuan peppercorns are known throughout China as 'flower peppers' because they look like flower buds opening. They are reddish brown in colour with a strong pungent odour, which distinguishes them from the hotter black peppercorns. Sichuan peppercorns are not from peppers at all, but are the dried berries of a shrub which is a member of the citrus family. I find their smell reminds me of lavender, while their taste is sharp and mildly spicy. They can be ground in a conventional peppermill and are very often roasted before grinding to bring out their full flavour. Sold wrapped in cellophane or plastic bags in Chinese grocers, Sichuan peppercorns are inexpensive. They will keep indefinitely if stored in a well-sealed container.

To roast Sichuan peppercorns
Heat a wok or heavy frying-pan to medium heat. Add the peppercorns (you can cook up to about 5 oz (150 g) at a time) and stir-fry for about 5 minutes until they brown slightly and start to smoke. Remove the pan from the heat and leave to cool. Grind the peppercorns in a peppermill, clean coffee grinder or with a pestle and mortar. Seal the mixture tightly in a screw-top jar to store. Alternatively, keep the whole roasted peppercorns in a well sealed container and grind them when required.

SICHUAN PRESERVED VEGETABLE
There are many types of Chinese pickled vegetables. One of the most popular is Sichuan preserved vegetable, a speciality of

Sichuan Province. This is the root of the mustard green which is pickled in salt and hot chillies. Another type is Sichuan preserved cabbage. Sold in tins in Chinese grocers, they give a pleasantly crunchy texture and spicy taste to dishes. Before using the pre-served vegetable, rinse in cold water and then slice or chop as required. Any unused vegetable should be transferred to a tightly covered jar and stored in the refrigerator where the preserved vegetable should keep indefinitely.

STAR ANISE

The star anise is a hard, star-shaped spice and is the seed-pod of the anise bush. (It is also known as Chinese anise or whole anise.) It is similar in flavour and fragrance to common aniseed but is more robust and liquorice-like. Star anise is an essential ingredient of five spice powder and is widely used in braised dishes to which it imparts a rich taste and fragrance. Sold in plastic packs in Chinese grocers, star anise should be stored in a tightly covered jar in a cool, dry place.

SUGAR

Sugar has been used in the cooking of savoury dishes in China for a thousand years. Properly employed, it helps balance the various flavours of sauces and other dishes. Chinese sugar comes in several forms: rock or yellow lump sugar, brown sugar slabs and as maltose or malt sugar. I particularly like to use rock sugar, which is rich and has a more subtle flavour than refined granulated sugar. It also gives a good lustre or glaze to braised dishes and sauces. You can buy this sugar in Chinese grocers, where it is usually sold in packets. You may need to break the lumps into smaller pieces with a wooden mallet or rolling pin. If you cannot find this, use white sugar or coffee sugar crystals (the amber, chunky kind) instead.

VINEGARS

Vinegars are widely used in Chinese, Southeast Asian and Japanese cooking. Unlike Western vinegars, they are usually made from rice. There are many varieties, ranging in flavour from the spicy and slightly tart to the sweet and pungent, and all can be bought from Chinese grocers. They are sold in bottles and will keep indefin-itely. If you cannot obtain Chinese vinegars, I suggest you use cider vinegar instead. Malt vinegar can be used, but its taste is stronger and more acidic.

Black rice vinegar

Black rice vinegar is very dark in colour and rich though mild in taste. It is used for braised dishes, noodles and sauces.

Red rice vinegar

Red rice vinegar is sweet and spicy in taste and is usually used as a dipping sauce for seafood.

White rice vinegar

White rice vinegar is clear and mild in flavour. It has a faint taste of glutinous rice and is used for sweet and sour dishes.

WUNTUN SKINS

Wuntun skins are made from egg and flour and can be bought fresh or frozen from Chinese grocers. They are thin pastry-like wrappings which can be stuffed with minced meat, vegetables or sweet fillings, and fried, steamed or used in soups. They are sold in little piles of $3\frac{1}{4}$ inch (8 cm) yellowish squares, wrapped in plastic. The number of squares or skins in a packet varies from about 30 to 36, depending upon the supplier. Fresh wuntun skins will keep for about 5 days if stored in clingfilm or a plastic bag in the refrigerator. If you are using frozen wuntun skins, just peel off the number you require and thaw thoroughly before you use them.

Equipment

Much of the equipment used in other oriental cookery is similar to the Chinese, so I will discuss traditional Chinese cooking equipment. While not essential for cooking Southeast Asian, Japanese or Chinese food, there are a few pieces of equipment which will make it very much easier. Most items can be bought very cheaply, especially if you seek out authentic implements from a Chinese or oriental grocer, and you can now find fairly good versions sold in many department stores.

WOK

The most useful piece of equipment is the wok, in which it is easier to toss foods quickly without spilling them. It also requires far less oil for deep-frying than a deep-fat fryer, although you may find the latter easier and safer to use. Another advantage is that the shape of the wok allows the heat to spread evenly over its surface, thus making for rapid cooking which is fundamental to stir-frying.

There are two types of wok: the Cantonese wok which has a short, rounded handle on either side, and the pau wok which has one long handle. The Cantonese wok is best for steaming and deep-frying since it can be set steadily onto a stand over the heat, and is easier to move when it is full of liquid. The pau wok is better for stir-frying since it is easier to shake over the heat with one hand while your free hand wields a long-handled spoon or spatula. It also distances you from the heat and hot oil and makes for more comfortable, safer frying. Woks with rounded bases should only be used on gas hobs. It is now possible to buy woks with flattish bottoms which are specifically designed for electric hobs, but can also be used with gas as well. Although these really defeat the purpose of the traditional design, which is to concentrate intense heat at the centre, they do have the advantage of having deeper sides than a frying-pan.

Choosing a wok

Choose a large wok – preferably about 12–14 inches (30.5–35.5 cm) in diameter, with good deep sides. Some woks on the market are too shallow and are no better than a large frying-pan. Clearly, it is easier to cook a small quantity in a large wok than to try to accommodate a large quantity in a small one. Select one which is heavy and, if possible, made of carbon steel rather than a light stainless steel or aluminium. The latter types tend to scorch. I do not like non-stick woks; not only are they more expensive, but they cannot be seasoned like an ordinary wok, and this seasoning adds to the flavour of the food. I also dislike electric woks because I find they do not heat up to a sufficiently high temperature and tend to be too shallow.

Seasoning a wok

All woks (except non-stick ones) need to be seasoned. Many need to be scrubbed first as well to remove the machine oil which is applied to the surface by the manufacturer to protect it in transit. This is the *only* time you will ever scrub your wok – unless you let it rust up. Scrub it with a cream cleanser and water to remove as much of the machine oil as possible. Then dry it and put it on the hob on a low heat. Add 2 tablespoons cooking oil and rub this over the inside of the wok using kitchen paper until the entire surface is lightly coated with oil. Heat the wok slowly for about 10–15 minutes and then wipe it thoroughly with more kitchen paper. The paper will become blackened. Repeat this process of coating, heating and wiping until the kitchen paper wipes clean. Your wok will darken and become well seasoned with use.

Cleaning a wok

Do not scrub a seasoned wok. Just wash it in plain water without detergent. Dry it thoroughly, preferably by putting it over a low heat for a few minutes before storing. This should prevent the wok from rusting, but if it does, scrub the rust off with a cream cleanser and repeat the seasoning process.

WOK ACCESSORIES

Wok stand

This is a metal ring or frame designed to keep a conventionally shaped wok steady on the hob, and is essential if you want to use your wok for steaming, deep-frying or braising. Stands come in two designs. One is a solid metal ring with about 6 ventilation holes. The other is a circular thin wire frame. If you have a gas cooker, *use only the latter type*, as the more solid design does not allow for sufficient ventilation and may lead to a build-up of gas which could put the flame out completely.

Wok lid

A wok lid is a dome-like cover, usually made from aluminium, which is used for steaming. It may come with the wok or it can be purchased separately from a Chinese grocer, but any large domed pan lid which fits snugly over the top of the wok can be used instead. Alternatively, you could use foil.

Spatula

A long-handled metal spatula shaped rather like a small shovel is ideal for scooping and tossing food in a wok. Any good long-handled spoon can be used instead.

Rack

If you use your wok or a large pan as a steamer you will need a wooden or metal rack or trivet to stand above the water level and support the plate of food to be steamed. Some woks are sold with a metal stand, but most Chinese grocers, department stores and hardware shops stock triangular wooden stands or round metal stands which can be used for this purpose. You can improvise a stand by using an empty, inverted tin can of suitable height.

DEEP-FAT FRYERS

These are very useful, and you may find them safer and easier to use for deep-frying than a wok. *The quantities of oil given in the recipes are based on the amount required for deep-frying in a wok. If you are using a deep-fat fryer instead you will need about double that amount, but never fill it more than half-full with oil.*

CLEAVERS

No self-respecting Chinese or Southeast Asian cook would be seen with a knife instead of a cleaver. These heavy choppers serve many purposes. They are used for all kinds of cutting, ranging from fine shredding to chopping up bones. A Chinese cook would usually have three types: a lightweight one with a narrow blade for cutting delicate foods including vegetables; a medium-weight one for general cutting, chopping and crushing purposes; and a heavy one for heavy-duty chopping. Of course, you can prepare Chinese food using good sharp knives, but if you decide to invest in a cleaver, you will be surprised at how easy it is to use. Choose a good quality stainless steel one and keep it sharp.

CHOPPING BOARD

The Chinese traditionally use a soft wood block for chopping, but these blocks are not only difficult to maintain, they also accumulate bacteria. Therefore, I prefer to use a hardwood or acrylic board. Both are strong, easy to clean and last indefinitely. There is so much chopping and slicing to be done when preparing food for Chinese-style cooking that it really is essential to have a large, steady cutting board. (For health reasons never cut cooked meat on a board which you have also used for chopping raw meat or poultry. Keep a separate board for this purpose.) Always clean your cutting boards properly after use. Vinegar or lemon work well.

STEAMERS

Bamboo steamers are among the most ancient of Chinese cooking utensils. These attractive round 'boxes' come in several sizes of which the 10 inch (25.5 cm) size is the most suitable for home use. Bamboo steamers are filled with food and placed on top of a pan or over a wok of boiling water. Clean damp muslin is sometimes placed over the open slats under the food to prevent sticking. A tight-fitting bamboo lid is put on top to prevent the steam escaping. One of the advantages of the design is that several steamers can be stacked on top of the other for multiple cooking. Bamboo steamers can be bought in Chinese grocers. (Alternatively, any European kind of wide, metal steamer can be used.) Before using a bamboo steamer for the first time, wash and steam it empty for about 5 minutes.

RICE COOKERS

Electric rice cookers are increasing in popularity. They cook rice perfectly and keep it warm throughout a meal. A rice cooker also has the advantage of freeing a burner or element, making for a less cluttered hob. They are relatively expensive, however, so unless you eat rice frequently I do not think they are worth the expense.

CHOPSTICKS

Chopsticks are not just used for eating in Chinese and Southeast Asian cooking (with the exception of Thais, who use forks). They are also used when cooking, for stirring, beating and whipping. Special long chopsticks are available for these purposes, but it is perfectly all right to use Western cooking implements instead.

Table chopsticks come in wood, plastic and, most luxurious of all, ivory or silver. They can be bought from many department stores, Chinese grocers and many Chinese restaurants or take-aways.

Techniques

The preparation of food before cooking is probably more important and more time-consuming in Chinese, Japanese and Southeast Asian cookery than in any other cuisine. However, because the subject of this book is vegetables and pasta, many of the recipes are simpler and easier to make than those dealing with meats and poultry. It is important, nonetheless, to have all ingredients properly prepared beforehand. In stir-frying, for example, the food must be chopped into small, well-shaped pieces. This will ensure even and quick cooking, and is especially important for vegetables so as to avoid overcooking. Foods prepared and cooked this way retain their natural textures and tastes. Another reason for careful cutting is to enhance the visual appeal of a dish. This is why most Chinese and Southeast Asian cuisines are so specific about cutting techniques, particularly where vegetables are concerned. The Chinese always use a cleaver (page 29) for these tasks, wielding it with skill and dexterity, but a sharp heavy knife can be used instead.

Chinese cookery is a sophisticated cuisine which involves a number of cooking methods which are relatively uncommon in the West; many of them have been adopted in other Southeast Asian cuisines. Sometimes several different cooking techniques are used in the preparation of a single dish, such as deep-frying bean-curd and then braising it. Most of these techniques can be easily mastered with a little practice. When you are planning a meal, be sure to select dishes which use a range of techniques; limit yourself to one stir-fried dish per meal until you have become used to this important method of cooking.

CUTTING TECHNIQUES
Slicing
This is the conventional method of slicing food. Hold the food firmly on the chopping board with one hand and slice the food straight down into very thin slices. If you use a cleaver rather than a knife for this, hold the cleaver with your index finger over the far side of the top of the cleaver and your thumb on the side nearest you

to guide the cutting edge firmly. Hold the food with your other hand, turning your fingers under for safety. Your knuckles should act as a guide for the blade.

Horizontal or flat slicing

There is a technique for splitting food into 2 thinner pieces while retaining its overall shape. It can be used for cutting beancurd in half, for example. The cleaver, with its wide blade, is particularly suitable for this. Hold the blade of the cleaver or knife parallel to the chopping board and place your free hand on top of the piece of food to keep it steady. Using a gentle cutting motion, slice horizontally through the food.

Diagonal slicing

This technique is used for cutting vegetables such as asparagus, carrots or spring onions. The purpose is to expose more of the surface of the vegetable for quicker cooking. Angle the knife or cleaver at a slant and cut.

Roll cutting

This is rather like diagonal slicing but is used for larger vegetables such as courgettes, large carrots, aubergines and Chinese white radish (mooli). As with diagonal slicing, this technique allows more of the surface of the vegetable to be exposed to the heat, thereby speeding up the cooking time. Begin by making one diagonal slice at one end of the vegetable. Then turn it 180 degrees and make the next diagonal slice. Continue in this way until you have chopped the entire vegetable into evenly sized, diamond-shaped chunks.

Shredding

This is the process by which food is cut into thin, fine, matchstick-like shreds. First cut the food into slices, then pile several slices on top of each other and cut them *lengthways* into fine strips.

Dicing

This is a simple technique of cutting food into small cubes or dice. The food should first be cut into slices. Stack the slices and cut them again *lengthways* into sticks just as you would for shredding (above). Stack the strips or sticks and cut *crossways* into evenly sized cubes or dice.

Scoring

This is a technique used to pierce the surface of foods to help them cook faster and more evenly. It also gives them an attractive appearance. Use a cleaver or sharp knife and make cuts into the food at a slight angle to a depth of about $\frac{1}{8}$ inch (0.3 cm). Take care not to cut all the way through. Make cuts all over the surface of the food, cutting criss-cross to give a wide, diamond-shaped pattern.

COOKING TECHNIQUES
Blanching
This involves putting food into hot water or into moderately hot oil for a few minutes to cook it briefly but not entirely. It is a sort of softening-up process to prepare the food for final cooking. Blanching in water is common with harder vegetables such as broccoli or carrots. The vegetable is plunged into boiling water for several minutes. It is then drained and plunged into cold water to arrest the cooking process. In such cases, blanching usually precedes stir-frying which completes the cooking.

Poaching
This is a method of simmering food until it is partially cooked. It is then put into soup or combined with a sauce and the cooking process continued.

Stir-frying
This is the most famous of all Chinese cooking techniques and is used extensively. It is possibly the most tricky technique since success with it depends upon having all the required ingredients prepared, measured out and immediately to hand, and on having a good source of fierce heat. Its advantage is that, properly executed, stir-fried foods can be cooked in minutes in very little oil so they retain their natural flavours and textures. It is very important that stir-fried foods should not be overcooked or greasy. Once you have mastered this technique you will find that it becomes almost second nature. Using a wok is definitely an advantage when stir-frying as its shape not only conducts the heat well but its high sides enable you to toss and stir ingredients rapidly, keeping them constantly moving while cooking. Having prepared all the ingredients for stir-frying, follow the steps below.

■ Heat the wok or frying-pan until it is very hot *before* adding the oil. This prevents food sticking and will ensure an even heat. Add the oil and, using a metal spatula or long-handled spoon, distribute it evenly over the surface. It should be very hot indeed – almost smoking – before you add the next ingredient unless you are going on to flavour the oil (see next point).

■ If you are flavouring the oil with garlic, spring onions, ginger, dried red chilli or other seasoning, do not wait for the oil to get so hot that it is almost smoking. If you do, these ingredients will burn and become bitter. Toss them quickly in the oil for a few seconds. In some recipes these flavourings will then be removed and discarded before cooking proceeds.

■ Now add the ingredients as described in the recipe and proceed to stir-fry by tossing them over the surface of the wok or pan with the metal spatula or long-handled spoon. Keep moving the food from the centre of the wok to the sides. Stir-frying is a noisy business and is usually accompanied by quite a lot of spluttering because of the high temperature at which the food must be cooked.

■ Some stir-fried dishes are thickened with a mixture of cornflour and cold water. To avoid getting a lumpy sauce be sure to remove the wok or pan from the heat before you add the cornflour mixture, which must be thoroughly blended before it is added. The sauce can then be returned to the heat and thickened.

Deep-frying

This is one of the most important techniques in Chinese cookery. The trick is to regulate the heat so that the surface of the food is sealed but does not brown so fast that the food is uncooked inside. Although deep-fried food must not be greasy, the process does require a lot of oil. The Chinese use a wok for deep-frying which requires rather less oil than a deep-fat fryer; however, I think you should avoid using a wok until you are very sure of it. When you do, be certain that it is fully secure on its stand before adding the oil or, if it is flat-bottomed, that it is secured on its own. On no account leave the wok unsupervised. Most people will find a deep-fat fryer easier and safer to use. Be careful not to fill this more than half-full with oil. Below are some points to bear in mind when deep-frying.

■ Wait for the oil to get hot enough before adding the food to be fried. The oil should give off a haze and almost produce little wisps of smoke when it is the right temperature, but you can test it by dropping in a small piece of food. If it bubbles all over then the oil is sufficiently hot. Adjust the heat as necessary to prevent the oil from actually smoking or overheating.

■ Be sure to dry food to be deep-fried thoroughly first with kitchen paper as this will prevent spluttering. If the food is in a marinade, remove it with a slotted spoon and drain before putting it into the oil. If you are using batter, make sure all the excess batter drips off before adding the food to the hot oil.

■ Oil used for deep-frying can be re-used. Cool it and then strain into a jar through several layers of muslin or through a fine mesh to remove any particles of food which might otherwise burn if reheated and give the oil a bitter taste. Label the jar according to what food you have cooked in the oil, and only re-use it for the same purpose. Oil can be used up to three times before it begins to lose its effectiveness.

Shallow-frying or pan-frying

This technique is similar to sautéeing. It involves more oil than stir-frying but less than for deep-frying. Food is fried first on one side and then on the other. Sometimes the excess oil is drained off and a sauce added to complete the dish. A frying-pan or a flat-bottomed wok is ideal for shallow-frying.

Slow-simmering and steeping

These processes are very similar. In slow-simmering, food is immersed in liquid which is brought almost to the boil and then the temperature is reduced so that it simmers, cooking the food to the desired degree. This is the technique used for making stock. In steeping, food is similarly immersed in liquid (usually stock) and simmered for a time. The heat is then turned off and the residual heat of the liquid finishes off the cooking process.

Braising and red-braising

These techniques are most often applied to certain vegetables. The food is usually browned or deep-fried and then put into stock which has been flavoured with seasonings and spices. The stock is brought to the boil, the heat reduced and the food simmered gently until it is cooked. Red-braising, which is also known as red-cooking, is simply the technique by which food is braised in a dark liquid such as soy sauce. This gives food a reddish brown colour, hence the name. This type of braising sauce can be saved and frozen for re-use. It can be re-used many times and becomes richer in flavour.

Steaming

Steaming has been used by the Chinese for thousands of years. Along with stir-frying and deep-frying, it is the most widely used technique. Steamed foods are cooked by a gentle moist heat which must circulate freely in order to cook the food. It is an excellent method for bringing out subtle flavours and so is particularly good for fish. Vegetables are almost never steamed; they are blanched instead. Bamboo steamers are used by the Chinese, but you could choose from a variety of utensils.

Using a bamboo steamer in a wok   For this you need a large bamboo steamer about 10 inches (25.5 cm) wide. Put about 2 inches (5 cm) of water in a wok and bring to simmering point. Put the bamboo steamer containing the food into the wok where it should rest safely perched on the sloping sides. Cover the steamer with its matching lid and steam the food until it is cooked. Replenish the water as required.

Using a wok as a steamer   Put about 2 inches (5 cm) water into a wok and then place a metal or wooden rack into the wok. Bring the water to simmering point and put the food to be steamed onto a heatproof plate. Lower the plate onto the rack and cover the wok tightly with the lid. Check the water level from time to time and replenish it with hot water when necessary.

Using a large roasting tin or pan as a steamer   Put a metal or wooden rack into the tin or pan and pour in about 2 inches (5 cm) water. Bring to simmering point and put the food to be steamed onto a heatproof plate. Lower the plate onto the rack and cover the tin or pan with a lid or foil. Replenish the water as necessary.

If you do not have a metal or wooden rack, you could use a small empty tin to support the plate of food. Remember that the food needs to remain above the water level and must not get wet. The water level should always be at least 1 inch (2.5 cm) below the edge of the plate. (Be sure to use a heatproof plate.)

Using a European steamer   If you have a metal steamer which is wide enough to take a plate of food then this will give you very satisfactory results. Keep an eye on the level of the water in the base.

Reheating foods

Steaming is one of the best methods of reheating food since it warms the food without cooking it further and without drying it out. To reheat soups and braised dishes, bring the liquid slowly to a simmer but do not boil. Remove it from the heat as soon as it is hot to prevent overcooking.

ONE

STARTERS & APPETISERS

Starters or appetisers are meant to stimulate the palate, to prepare one for the offerings to come. As such, I like them to be subtly appealing in taste and textures. In most cases they should be simple and light, for you don't wish to overwhelm the main course. And yet some appetisers, like Northern Chinese Vegetable Potstickers, are almost a meal in themselves. Indeed, it is not uncommon when dining out in a Chinese restaurant to see people make their selections only from the starters section of the menu. The rule here is to make and use the recipes as they fit into your meal or menu. They may be used as starters; as a first course in a series of courses; or as a part of many courses – that is, if you wish to follow the Chinese custom of including different courses on the table at once; or you may serve them as another dish in a family meal. Use these starters with all styles of cookery, not just Chinese. Be imaginative – combine or match these appetisers with other foods and beverages, or serve them as mini meals in themselves.

THAI SWEETCORN PANCAKES

Sweetcorn is one of the numerous 'New World' vegetables – along with tomatoes, white and sweet potatoes, peppers, chillies – introduced relatively recently into China and Southeast Asia and now extremely popular ingredients in these cuisines. Thai cookery often uses sweetcorn in its dishes and these hot and spicy pancakes are typical of Thai food. I prefer it even hotter, but if you wish you may cut down on the chillies. Delicious served warm or cold, these pancakes make an excellent starter but may also be served as a side vegetable dish to a main course.

Serves 4 to 6

2 lb (900 g) fresh sweetcorn on the cob, or 20 oz
  (550 g) tinned sweetcorn
2 eggs, beaten
1 tablespoon cornflour
2 tablespoons chopped fresh coriander
1 tablespoon finely chopped garlic
2 tablespoons finely chopped fresh ginger
$\frac{1}{4}$ teaspoon black pepper
1 teaspoon salt
2 tablespoons coarsely chopped fresh chillies
1 tablespoon oil, preferably groundnut

Remove the corn kernels from the cob with a sharp knife or cleaver. You should end up with about $1\frac{1}{4}$ lb (550 g). If you are using tinned sweetcorn, empty the contents and drain thoroughly. Set aside half of the sweetcorn in a separate bowl. Combine the rest of the corn with the remaining ingredients, except the oil. Purée the mixture in a blender, then fold in the reserved corn.

Heat a frying-pan, preferably non-stick, add the oil and spoon in 2 tablespoons of the mixture. Cook the pancake over medium heat for 2–3 minutes or until golden brown on one side. Using a knife or spatula, turn the pancake over and cook the other side until crisp and golden. Remove, drain on kitchen paper and keep warm. Continue until you have used up all the mixture.

CHINESE PANCAKES
Photograph between pages 112 and 113

These are simply flour-and-water pancakes with no seasonings or spices at all. As such, they blend perfectly with a variety of dishes such as Mu-Shu Vegetables (page 96), and serve as the basis of other dishes such as Spring Onion Pancakes (page 40). They are used like bread in the West. Once you have acquired the knack – practice, practice – they are easy to make. The unusual method of rolling 'double' pancakes is designed to ensure thinner, moister pancakes with less chance of being overcooked. Because they can be frozen, it is possible to make a batch many days, even weeks, ahead of time. Thaw thoroughly before steaming them. These pancakes can be used with practically any stir-fried dish which does not contain too much sauce.

Makes about 18 pancakes

10 oz (275 g) plain flour
8–9 fl oz (225–250 ml) very hot water
2 tablespoons sesame oil

Put the flour into a large bowl. Stir the hot water gradually into the flour, mixing continuously with chopsticks or a fork until the water is fully incorporated. Add more water if the mixture seems dry. Remove the mixture from the bowl and knead it with your hands. Return it to the bowl, cover with a clean, damp tea towel and leave to rest for about 30 minutes.

After the resting period, take the dough out of the bowl and knead again for about 5 minutes, dusting with a little flour if sticky. Once the dough is smooth, form it into a roll about 18 inches (45.5 cm) long and about 1 inch (2.5 cm) in diameter. Take a knife and cut the roll into equal pieces. There should be about eighteen. Roll each piece into a ball.

Take 2 of the dough balls. Dip one side of one ball into the sesame oil and place the oiled side on top of the other ball. Using a rolling pin, roll the 2 pancakes simultaneously into a circle about 6 inches (15 cm) in diameter. It is important to roll double pancakes in this way because the resulting dough will remain moist inside and you will be able to roll them thinner, but avoid the risk of overcooking them later. Place a frying-pan or wok over a very low heat. Put the double pancake into the pan and cook until dried on one side. Flip the pancakes over and cook the other side. Remove from the pan, peel the 2 pancakes apart and set aside. Repeat this process until all the dough balls have been cooked.

Steam the pancakes to reheat them, or alternatively you could wrap them tightly in a double sheet of foil and put into a pan containing 1 inch (2.5 cm) boiling water. Cover the pan, turn the heat down very low and simmer until they are reheated. Don't be tempted to reheat the pancakes in the oven as this will dry them out too much. If you want to freeze the cooked pancakes, wrap them tightly in freezer wrap first. When using pancakes which have been frozen, let them thaw in the refrigerator first before reheating.

SPRING ONION PANCAKES

Pancakes are familiar items in practically every cuisine. This particular type is popular in northern China, where winters are cold and harsh. They are slightly doughy and heavy but are nonetheless delicious and especially appropriate on cold winter days. In China, they are eaten with noodle soup or rice gruel in the mornings. Western habits and palates find them more suitable as starters or snacks with drinks. Pan-fried in oil with spring onion and sesame oil, these pancakes have an enticing, pungent aroma that gives the appetite an edge. They should be consumed while still warm. Although I like to use them as a starter, they are equally good as a snack with a bowl of hot soup or noodles. Use a non-stick pan and experiment with using as little oil as possible. The authentic original version is slightly too oily for my taste.

Makes about 8 pancakes

pancake dough (page 39)
8 spring onions, finely chopped
1 tablespoon salt
1 tablespoon sesame oil
2–3 tablespoons oil, preferably groundnut

Make up the pancake dough according to the recipe for Chinese Pancakes (page 39). After the resting time, take the dough out of the bowl and knead it again for about 5 minutes, dusting with a little flour if sticky. Add the spring onions, salt and sesame oil, and knead the dough well.

Divide the dough into 8 equal pieces. Roll each piece into a circle about 6 inches (15 cm) in diameter.

Place a non-stick frying-pan or wok over a low heat. Add enough oil to lightly coat the bottom of the pan. Put the pancakes into the pan, making sure the edges do not touch, and cook until the pancakes are crispy on one side. Flip them over and cook on the other side. You may have to do this in several batches. Cut each one into 6 wedges and serve at once.

SUGAR WALNUTS

Walnuts, native to Asia, Europe and North America, hardly need an introduction. As might be expected, there are many ways of using them in the various cuisines of the world. Here, I have added the distinctive flavours of anise and cinnamon – walnuts are hearty enough to handle them, even though the blanching process has moderated the walnuts' slight bitterness. Cooking them in the syrup and allowing them to dry gives the walnuts a tasty coating and seals in the syrup flavours. Delicious served as a starter with drinks, these walnuts are also used in the recipe for Crispy Cabbage with Sugar Walnuts (page 42), forming a classic combination of sweet and salty tastes, and crunchy and delicate crispness.

Once deep-fried, the walnuts can be stored in a tightly covered glass jar for at least one week. The recipe can easily be doubled.

Serves 2 to 4

4 oz (110 g) walnuts, shelled
10 fl oz (300 ml) oil, preferably groundnut, for deep-frying

Syrup

15 fl oz (400 ml) water
2 oz (50 g) sugar
2 star anise
1 cinnamon stick or Chinese cinnamon bark
3 tablespoons honey

Preheat the oven to its lowest temperature, then switch off.

Bring a saucepan of water to the boil. Add the walnuts and cook for 2 minutes to blanch. Drain the nuts in a colander or sieve.

Mix the syrup ingredients together in a pan. Combine the nuts with the syrup mixture and boil for 10 minutes or until the syrup mixture thickens. Remove the nuts with a slotted spoon, place on a baking tray and leave to dry in the oven for at least 2 hours.

Heat the oil in a deep-fat fryer or wok to moderate heat. Fry a batch of walnuts for about 2 minutes or until the walnuts turn dark brown (watch the heat to prevent burning). Remove the walnuts with a slotted spoon or strainer and lay them on a baking tray to cool. Deep-fry and drain the rest of the walnuts in the same way. Serve them warm with Crispy Cabbage or cold with drinks.

CRISPY CABBAGE WITH SUGAR WALNUTS

Photograph opposite page 80

This is a popular vegetable starter in many Chinese restaurants in the UK, where it is known as 'Fried Seaweed'. In northern China, as I understand, there is a true seaweed dish to be had (which I have never eaten), but I should be very much surprised if it is available here. In my experience, the 'seaweed' is shredded, dried and deep-fried fresh Chinese greens. The taste is fine but I prefer the version offered here, from the Sichuan Garden restaurant in Hong Kong. It uses a tinned preserved cabbage called 'red-in-snow' which is a pickled vegetable, traditional among the people of Chekiang and Kiangsu in northern China. It looks like turnip tops and both leaves and stalks are preserved. In the late winter or early spring, the red roots of the plant are often visible through the snow, hence its name. If you cannot find it, use Chinese green leaves, finely shredded and thoroughly dried in the oven. The key to the success of this dish is to be sure that the red-in-snow cabbage is thoroughly dried and the oil quite hot. Serve the dish at once.

Serves 4

6½ oz (182 g) tinned red-in-snow cabbage
10 fl oz (300 ml) oil, preferably groundnut, for deep-frying
Sugar Walnuts (page 41)

Rinse the cabbage in several changes of cold water. Place on a
linen tea towel and squeeze out all the excess liquid.
  Heat the oil into a deep-fat fryer or wok until it almost smokes.
Deep-fry half of the cabbage for about 3 minutes or until crispy,
then drain on kitchen paper. Repeat the process with the remaining
cabbage. Mix the walnuts with the cabbage and serve at once.

HOT AND SPICY WALNUTS

This is a spicy, savoury way to prepare walnuts to be served either
as a snack with drinks or as a crunchy addition to other stir-fry
dishes. Prepared this way, the walnuts lend themselves to many
uses; use your imagination and experiment with them. You may
want to try them with Crispy Cabbage (opposite) instead of using
the sugar walnuts. If the walnuts get soft before they are used,
you may recrisp them by heating in a warm oven. They can be
made ahead of time but should be eaten within a few days of their
preparation. They do not keep for a long time because of the
seasonings used in this recipe.

Serves 4 to 6

8 oz (225 g) walnuts, shelled
2 tablespoons chilli bean sauce
1 tablespoon finely chopped garlic
1 tablespoon finely chopped fresh ginger
3 tablespoons Chinese black rice vinegar or cider vinegar
2 tablespoons sugar
2 tablespoons dark soy sauce
2 tablespoons Chinese white rice vinegar or cider vinegar
1¼ pints (700 ml) water
15 fl oz (400 ml) oil, preferably groundnut, for deep-frying

Garnish
3 tablespoons finely chopped spring onions

Bring a saucepan of water to the boil. Add the walnuts and simmer
for about 5 minutes to blanch. Drain the nuts in a colander or
sieve, then pat dry with kitchen paper.

Combine all the remaining ingredients together in a saucepan. Add the walnuts and cook for about 20 minutes over high heat. Drain the nuts and spread them on a baking tray. Leave to dry for at least 2 hours or more.

Heat the oil in a deep-fat fryer or wok to a moderate heat. Fry some of the walnuts for about 3 minutes or until they turn deep brown and crispy. (Watch the heat to prevent burning.) You may have to deep-fry them in several batches. Remove the walnuts with a slotted spoon or strainer and drain on kitchen paper. Allow them to cool and become crisp before serving. Garnish with the spring onions.

VIETNAMESE-STYLE VEGETARIAN SPRING ROLLS

Spring rolls are very much a Chinese dish but, to my taste, the Vietnamese version is the best. They are made with rice paper wrappers instead of flour pancakes, and this renders them lighter and crisper. I like the traditional practice of wrapping the cooked spring rolls in a fresh lettuce leaf with mint, basil or fresh coriander leaves and dipping them in a spicy peanut sauce. Such spring rolls are a splendid opener to any meal. The rice paper wrappers can be found in Chinese or oriental grocers. They are dry and must be gently soaked before using them. Handle them with care as they are quite fragile. When deep-frying the spring rolls, do not crowd them in the pan as they tend to stick.

Makes about 25 small spring rolls

1 packet rice paper wrappers
15 fl oz (400 ml) oil, preferably groundnut, for deep-frying

Stuffing
2 oz (50 g) bean thread (transparent) noodles
2 oz (50 g) carrots, finely shredded
4 oz (110 g) mange-tout, finely shredded
3 tablespoons finely chopped spring onions
1 teaspoon sesame oil
2 tablespoons light soy sauce
1 teaspoon Chinese rice wine or dry sherry

To serve
8 oz (225 g) iceberg lettuce
assorted sprigs of basil, mint or coriander, or a combination of all three
Spicy Peanut Sauce (page 46)

For the stuffing, soak the noodles in a large bowl of warm water for 15 minutes. When they are soft, drain and discard the water. Cut the noodles into 3 inch (7.5 cm) lengths, using scissors or a knife.

In a large bowl, mix the noodles with the carrots, mange-tout, spring onions, sesame oil, light soy sauce and rice wine.

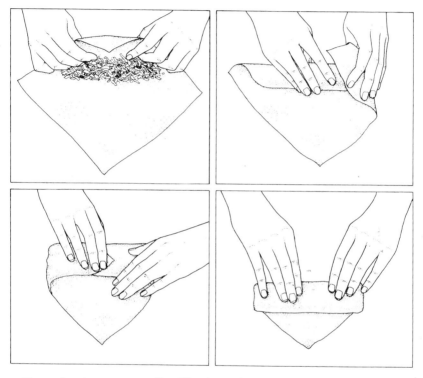

To make the spring rolls, fill a large bowl with warm water and dip one of the rice paper wrappers in the water to soften. Remove and drain on a linen tea towel. Put about 2 tablespoons of the filling on each softened rice paper wrapper. Fold in each side and then roll up tightly. They will seal by themselves. You should have a roll about 3 inches (7.5 cm) long, a little like a small sausage. Repeat the procedure until you have used up all the filling.

Heat the oil in a deep-fat fryer or large wok until it is hot. Deep-fry the spring rolls, a few at a time, until golden brown, about 2 minutes. They have a tendency to stick to each other at the beginning of the frying, so only fry a few at a time. Drain on kitchen paper. Serve at once with lettuce leaves, herb sprigs and peanut dipping sauce (page 46).

SPICY PEANUT SAUCE

Dipping sauces are common in all Far Eastern cuisines. Here is a tasty Southeast Asian version, commonly used with spring rolls. It has a peanut flavour but the secret charm of this dip lies in the addition of fish sauce, an essential ingredient which you should try to obtain. You may adjust the chilli oil to suit your own palate. This sauce may be made well ahead of time.

Makes enough for about 25 small spring rolls

1 tablespoon fish sauce
2 tablespoons Chinese white rice vinegar or cider vinegar
$\frac{1}{2}$ teaspoon finely chopped garlic
3 tablespoons roasted peanuts, coarsely chopped
1 teaspoon chilli oil
2 tablespoons water
1 teaspoon sugar

Combine all the ingredients together in a small bowl, mixing them thoroughly. Leave the dipping sauce to stand for at least 10 minutes before using.

NORTHERN CHINESE VEGETABLE POTSTICKERS

Potstickers are a form of dumpling and, in northern China, they are a speciality in restaurants and a staple in home kitchens. To this day, making them is a family affair and social occasion, with Sunday mornings before the big lunch meal devoted to their preparation. In general, dumplings may be shallow-fried, boiled, poached or steamed. One very popular way to make them is to shallow-fry in oil and water until they literally stick to the pan, a method I like best of all. Properly done, it produces true potsticker dumplings that are crisp on the bottom, soft on the top and juicy inside. The goal is to have a contrast of textures and flavours.

In China, potsticker dumplings usually include minced pork. Here, I omit the pork and offer a vegetarian one that is completely satisfying. Try to obtain the Chinese preserved vegetables and Chinese chives; they add an excellent flavour to the dumplings. You may substitute ordinary chives, but there is really no substitute for the preserved vegetables. Make your own dipping sauce with chilli oil, dark soy sauce and Chinese white rice vinegar or cider vinegar.

Potsticker dumplings may be frozen uncooked and can be transferred directly from the freezer to the pan; just cook them a little longer than usual. Ready-made potsticker wrappers can be found in Chinese grocers if you choose not to make your own.

Makes about 20 dumplings

1 packet potsticker wrappers, bought or made according to the recipe below

Dough
5 oz (150 g) plain flour
4 fl oz (110 ml) very hot water

Stuffing
4 oz (110 g) fresh or frozen peas
2 oz (50 g) Sichuan preserved vegetables, finely chopped
2 tablespoons finely chopped garlic
8 oz (225 g) bok choy, finely chopped
8 oz (225 g) Chinese chives, coarsely chopped
¼ teaspoon salt
pinch freshly ground pepper
2 tablespoons rice wine or dry sherry
1 tablespoon dark soy sauce
2 teaspoons sugar
3 tablespoons oil, preferably groundnut
5 fl oz (150 ml) water

If you are making the dough, put the flour into a large bowl and gradually stir in the hot water, mixing continuously with a fork or chopsticks until most of the water is incorporated. Add more water if the mixture seems dry. Remove the dough from the bowl and knead with your hands until smooth. This should take about 5 minutes. Put the dough back into the bowl, cover with a clean, damp teatowel and leave to rest for about 20 minutes.

While the dough is resting, make the stuffing. If you are using fresh peas, blanch them in a pan of boiling water for 4 minutes or 2 minutes if they are frozen. Rinse the Sichuan preserved vegetables several times in cold water and blot them dry.

Heat a wok or large frying-pan over high heat and add 1 tablespoon of the oil. Add the stuffing ingredients and stir-fry for 5 minutes or until the mixture is dry. Remove the mixture to a bowl and allow the stuffing ingredients to cool thoroughly.

After the resting time, take the dough out of the bowl and knead it again for about 5 minutes, dusting with a little flour if sticky. Once the dough is smooth, form into a roll about 9 inches (23 cm) long and about 1 inch (2.5 cm) in diameter. Take a knife and cut the roll into 18 equal pieces.

Roll each piece of dough into a small ball, then roll each ball into a small, round, flat 'pancake' about $2\frac{1}{2}$ inches (6 cm) in diameter. Arrange the rounds on a lightly floured tray and cover with damp kitchen paper to keep them from drying out until required.

Put about 1 tablespoon of the filling in the centre of each pancake, then fold in half. Moisten the edges with water and pinch together with your fingers. Pleat around the edge, pinching to seal well.

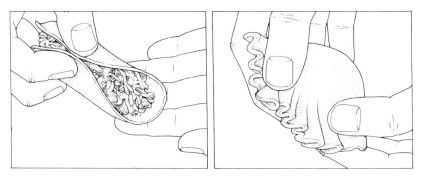

Transfer the finished dumplings to the floured tray and keep it covered with a damp cloth until you have filled all the dumplings in this way.

Heat a frying pan (preferably non-stick) over a high heat until hot and add 1 tablespoon of the oil. Place the dumplings, flat side down, into the pan. Turn down the heat and cook for about 2 minutes until lightly browned. (You may need to cook the dumplings in 2 batches.) Add the 5 fl oz (150 ml) water, cover the pan tightly and cook for about 12 minutes or until most of the liquid is absorbed. Uncover the pan and continue to cook for a further 2 minutes. Remove the dumplings and serve.

Place three bowls on the table, containing Chinese white rice vinegar, chilli oil and dark soy sauce. Let each person concoct their own dipping sauce by mixing these three items exactly to their taste.

WINTER VEGETABLE FRITTERS

These vegetable fritters (similar to pancakes), served warm or at room temperature, are an appetising starter for any meal. You may substitute other vegetables as long as they are firm, such as cucumbers or courgettes. The key ingredient in this version is fresh waterchestnuts – try to obtain them, for they add a special sweetness and texture to the fritters. Served with a simple green salad, these vegetable fritters also make a delicious light lunch.

Serves 2 to 4

4 oz (110 g) carrots
4 oz (110 g) fresh or tinned waterchestnuts
4 oz (110 g) cabbage
1 small onion
6 tablespoons plain flour
1 tablespoon cornflour
3 eggs, beaten
2 teaspoons salt
2 teaspoons baking powder
2 teaspoons sugar
1 teaspoon freshly ground black pepper
3–4 tablespoons oil, preferably groundnut

Finely chop the carrots, waterchestnuts, cabbage and onion. Lightly blend all the ingredients, except the oil, in a food processor or food mill for a few seconds. Do not use a blender.

Heat a frying-pan or wok and add the oil. Spoon in 3 tablespoons of the mixture to make a 4 inch (10 cm) wide pancake and fry for 2–3 minutes or until golden brown on one side. Using a knife or spatula, turn the pancake over and cook the other side until crispy and golden. Continue this process until you have used up all the mixture. Cut the fritters into wedges and serve.

CRISPY VEGETARIAN WUNTUNS
Photograph opposite page 80

Wuntuns stuffed with tasty fillings of flavourful vegetables or meat are universally appreciated. This is a vegetarian version of the traditional Chinese treat with a filling of carrots, cabbage and bean sprouts, with some beancurd for body. These wuntuns are delicious with hoisin sauce or, if you prefer, a dipping sauce made with your own combination of chilli oil, white rice wine vinegar and light soy sauce. These wuntuns are ideal with drinks or as a starter.

Do *not* make them too far ahead of time. Because they are made with a moisture-laden vegetable stuffing, the wuntun skins will soften in an unpalatable way if they are allowed to stand for a long time. If possible, make and serve them straight away.

Makes 30 to 35 wuntuns

1 packet wuntun skins (about 30–35)
15 fl oz (400 ml) oil, preferably groundnut, for deep-frying
hoisin sauce, for dipping

Filling
1 tablespoon oil, preferably groundnut
2 oz (50 g) carrots, finely shredded
4 oz (110 g) cabbage, finely shredded
2 oz (50 g) bean sprouts
2 tablespoons finely chopped garlic
1 tablespoon dark soy sauce
3 tablespoons mashed beancurd
1 teaspoon sugar
$\frac{1}{2}$ teaspoon salt
1 teaspoon sesame oil
$\frac{1}{2}$ teaspoon freshly ground black pepper

For the filling, heat a wok or large frying-pan and add the oil. When moderately hot, add the carrots, cabbage, bean sprouts and garlic and stir-fry for 1 minute. Set aside to cool thoroughly.

Combine the cooled vegetables with the rest of the filling ingredients and mix well. Using a teaspoon, put a small amount of filling in the centre of each wuntun skin. Bring up 2 opposite corners, dampen the edges with a little water and pinch them together to

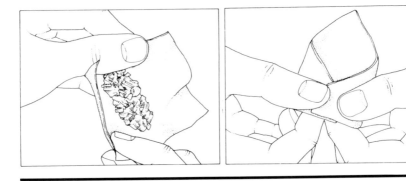

make a triangle. Fold over the bottom 2 corners so they overlap, and press together. The filling should be well sealed in.

Heat the oil in a deep-fat fryer or large wok until hot. Deep-fry the filled wuntuns in several batches. Drain on kitchen paper. Serve at once with hoisin sauce.

AUBERGINES WITH SESAME SAUCE

This is a very easy and delicious way to prepare aubergines. Try to obtain the smaller, more delicately flavoured Chinese aubergines if you can. The cooking process produces sweet, tender and moist aubergine flesh, and increases its receptivity to the classic Sichuan sauce: garlic, ginger and spring onions. This dish makes a delicious starter and, as it is served cold, may be made hours in advance. The sauce, however, should not be poured over the cooked aubergines until just before serving.

Serves 4

$1\frac{1}{2}$ lb (700 g) Chinese or ordinary aubergines

Sauce
1 tablespoon sesame paste
$\frac{1}{2}$ teaspoon roasted Sichuan peppercorns (page 24)
2 tablespoons sesame oil
2 teaspoons chilli oil
2 teaspoons sugar
1 teaspoon Chinese white rice vinegar or cider vinegar
$\frac{1}{2}$ teaspoon finely chopped garlic
$\frac{1}{2}$ teaspoon finely chopped fresh ginger
2 tablespoons finely chopped spring onions
1 tablespoon dark soy sauce

Preheat the oven to Gas Mark 6, 400°F (200°C). Put the aubergines in a roasting tin and bake for about 30 minutes if they are the Chinese variety or 45 minutes if they are the larger variety. They should be charred outside and tender inside. Allow them to cool thoroughly.

Peel the aubergines and shred the flesh or cut into strips. Arrange the aubergines on a serving plate.

Mix all the sauce ingredients together in a small bowl. Just before serving, pour the sauce over the aubergine.

SPICY KOREAN KIMCHI

Pickled vegetables are a speciality in Chinese and Southeast Asian cuisines. This is understandable, given the abundance of vegetables on the one hand and the absence of refrigeration (until quite recently) on the other. Necessity generated inventiveness and imagination to preserve the foods in a palatable way. Korean meals almost always include a pickled vegetable, 'kimchi' as it is called generically, to stimulate the palate and as a contrast to less fiery foods. In the West, we use our pickled dishes more sparingly, serving them on picnics or with cold platters. In this adaptation of Korean kimchi, I follow the traditional method of fermentation without the use of vinegar. The leaves develop a slightly sour taste enlivened by chilli – if you find it too hot, reduce the amount of chilli. Pickled cabbage is sold in glass jars in specialist food shops but it is usually full of preservatives and monosodium glutamate. I urge you to make your own; it is quite simple, can be prepared in advance, and keeps for weeks in the refrigerator.

Makes about 1 lb (450 g)

1 lb (450 g) Chinese leaves
2 tablespoons salt
2 pints (1.1 ltr) cold water
1 pint (570 ml) very hot water

Pickling mixture
1 tablespoon finely chopped garlic
1 tablespoon finely chopped fresh ginger
1 tablespoon finely chopped spring onions
2 teaspoons finely chopped dried chilli
2 teaspoons sugar
1 tablespoon salt

Separate the leaves and sprinkle them with the salt. Pour in the cold water and leave to stand in a cool place for 8 hours or overnight. Rinse the cabbage well and squeeze out the excess liquid.

Boil the water and pour over the pickling mixture. Mix well and combine with the Chinese leaves. Put the leaves with the pickling mixture into a large glass bowl. You may have to cut the leaves in half to make them fit. Cover the kimchi with cling film and leave in a cool place for about 2 days. Drain and cut the leaves into bite-size pieces. Pack into a glass jar until ready to serve.

JAPANESE-STYLE MARINATED MUSHROOMS

What could be easier than a dish that requires no cooking? Well, almost no cooking: the marinade must be heated and it in turn 'cooks' the mushrooms overnight. This simple and delicious starter also makes a splendid side dish for roasted meats.

Serves 4

1 lb (450 g) small button mushrooms

Marinade
5 fl oz (150 ml) sake, rice wine or dry sherry
2 tablespoons light soy sauce
2 teaspoons sugar
1 tablespoon Chinese white rice vinegar or cider vinegar
½ teaspoon salt

Garnish
2 tablespoons finely chopped spring onions

Place the marinade ingredients in a small pan and simmer for about 5 minutes. Allow to cool thoroughly. Combine the cooled marinade with the whole mushrooms and leave to marinate overnight.

When ready to serve the mushrooms, drain them and discard the marinade. Garnish with the spring onions.

CRUNCHY RADISH SALAD

Looking like long, overgrown white carrots, these radishes are a staple in Chinese cookery. I have seen them referred to as icicle radish, Chinese turnip and rettish. Here, they are known as mooli or Chinese white radish. They are never eaten raw in China, but I enjoy their crunchy texture, especially in salads such as this. They have a mild peppery taste which is muted by cooking them; in this recipe, they are salted to remove the bite. Once this is done, the radishes lend themselves very well to other spices and seasonings, as in this Chinese dressing of soy sauce, sugar, pepper and sesame oil. Remember that the cool crunchy bite of Chinese radishes works well with Western type dressings, so do experiment. If you cannot obtain the Chinese version, substitute ordinary radishes but cut them in half to show off their whiteness and expose them to the dressing. (Salting ordinary radishes is optional.)

Serves 2 to 4

12 oz (350 g) Chinese white radish (mooli)
2 teaspoons salt

Dressing
$\frac{1}{4}$ teaspoon roasted Sichuan peppercorns (page 24)
1 tablespoon light soy sauce
1 teaspoon sugar
1 tablespoon sesame oil

Cut the radish into 3 inch (7.5 cm) long, $\frac{1}{4}$ inch (0.5 cm) thick pieces. Salt the pieces, toss to mix thoroughly and set aside for 20 minutes. Rinse the radish and pat dry with kitchen paper.

For the dressing, first roast the peppercorns. Combine all the dressing ingredients and pour over the radish. Mix thoroughly and serve.

SOUPS

Soup is excellent either to start a meal or as a meal in itself. In China and Southeast Asia, soups are often served as part of a meal, as one of the courses on the table; it also serves as a beverage. In this book, there are two types of soups: hearty and rich, such as Fiery Sichuan Soup or Sizzling Rice Soup; and light, brothy ones such as Tangy Tomato Soup with Lemongrass or Steamed Vegetable Soup. They may be used either as part of an oriental menu or in your everyday meals. Many are simple and easy to put together, especially if you have the stock already prepared.

The key to *any* good soup is the stock. It is virtually impossible to have a good soup without it. Although it takes a little effort and work to make a good stock, the rewards make it well worthwhile. Many of the soups in this book are based on either chicken or vegetable stock. The Japanese recipes use 'dashi', a fish-based stock (page 16), but chicken or vegetable stock can be substituted.

CHICKEN STOCK

Good stock is essential to all cuisines. This is especially true for a cuisine that relies upon vegetables and pasta. Because of its lightness, flavour and versatility, chicken stock should be considered a staple like salt, cooking oil or soy sauce. There are commercially prepared tinned or cubed stocks but many of them are inferior in quality, being too salty or containing additives and colourants. Try to make your own, as the best chicken stock is home-made. I usually make up a large batch of it and freeze in smaller portions for future use. Remember – *stock is the foundation of all good cooking.* Here are a few rules to remember when making chicken stock:

■ It is best to use 50 per cent bones and 50 per cent meat. Without meat, the stock will not have the necessary body, richness or depth. Stewing (old) hens are best, because they are inexpensive (if you can find them) and full of flavour.

■ Stock should simmer. Never let the stock come to the boil because that will result in a cloudy and heavy stock. Good flavour and digestibility come with a clear stock.

■ Use a deep heavy saucepan so the liquid covers all the solids and evaporation is slow.

■ Simmer on low heat and gently skim the stock every now and then to remove any impurities.

▨ Strain the stock slowly through several layers of muslin or a fine mesh strainer.

▨ Allow the stock to cool thoroughly before freezing.

If you make a habit of saving your uncooked chicken bones and carcasses, you will have the essential ingredient for stock in no time. It also makes good economic sense.

Makes about 7 pints (4 ltr)

6 lb (2.75 kg) chicken pieces, bones (backs, feet, wings, etc.)
7 pints (4 ltr) cold water
4 slices fresh ginger
4 spring onions
4 large garlic cloves
2 teaspoons Sichuan peppercorns, unroasted
2 teaspoons black peppercorns
$\frac{1}{2}$ teaspoon salt

Put the chicken pieces and bones into a very large saucepan. (The bones can be put in either frozen or defrosted.) Cover with the cold water and bring to simmering point.

Meanwhile, cut the ginger into diagonal slices, $2 \times \frac{1}{2}$ inch (5×1 cm). Remove the green tops from the spring onions. Lightly crush the garlic cloves leaving the skins on.

Using a large, flat spoon, gently skim off the scum as it rises from the bones. Watch the heat as the stock should *never* boil. Keep skimming until the stock looks clear. This can take from 20–40 minutes. Do not stir or disturb the stock.

Reduce the heat to a gentle simmer. Add the ginger, white parts of the spring onions, garlic, peppercorns and salt. Simmer the stock over a very low heat for between 2 and 4 hours, skimming any fat off the top at least twice during this time. The stock should be rich and full-bodied, which is why it needs to be simmered for such a long time. This way the stock (and any soup you make with it) will have plenty of flavour.

Strain the stock through several layers of dampened muslin or through a very fine mesh strainer. Leave to cool thoroughly. Remove any fat which has risen to the top. It is now ready to be used or transferred to containers and frozen for future use.

VEGETABLE STOCK

I prefer chicken stock to any other but I include this vegetable stock as an alternative. Vegetarian cooking presents a problem when it comes to stock. In the absence of poultry, fish or meat, it is difficult to prepare a rich stock, the foundation of any cuisine. Vegetable stocks tend to be comparatively weak and lack robustness. Even in China, the custom has been to add the additive monosodium glutamate to vegetable stock. Another popular vegetable stock employs the peppery bite of white radish to impart body to it. With my colleague Gordon Wing, I have experimented and found that cooking the vegetables in oil *before* simmering helps to impart flavour to the stock. Gordon suggests using dried Chinese mushrooms to add richness and depth. If you find the portions too large for your needs, cut the recipe in half.

Makes about 8 pints (4.5 ltr)

1 oz (25 g) Chinese dried mushrooms
2 lb (900 g) carrots
4 celery sticks
2 lb (900 g) onions
4 leeks
8 oz (225 g) shallots
2 tablespoons oil, preferably groundnut
6 spring onions
6 slices fresh ginger
8 garlic cloves, peeled and crushed
1 tablespoon black peppercorns
1 tablespoon Sichuan peppercorns
4 bay leaves
2 tablespoons salt
8 pints (4.5 ltr) water
3 tablespoons light soy sauce

If you are using dried mushrooms, soak them in warm water for 20 minutes. Drain, squeeze out any excess liquid and coarsely chop the mushroom caps and stalks.

Coarsely chop the carrots, celery and onions. Wash, cut and discard the green part of the leeks and coarsely chop the white portion. Peel the shallots but leave them whole.

Heat a large saucepan or wok over moderate heat and add the oil. Put in the spring onions, ginger, garlic and shallots, and stir-fry for 1 minute. Then add the carrots, celery, leeks and onions and continue to cook for 5 minutes. Put all the vegetables and the rest of the ingredients into a very large pan. Cover them with the cold water and bring to simmering point.

Using a large, flat spoon, skim off the foam as it rises to the top, this will take about 5 minutes. Bring the stock to the boil. Reduce the heat to moderate and simmer for about 2 hours.

Strain the stock through a large colander, then through a very fine mesh strainer. Leave to cool thoroughly. It is now ready to be used or transferred to containers and frozen for future use.

SOFT BEANCURD AND SPINACH SOUP

This simple but delicious and nutritious soup is easy to prepare and one you would often find on the table in China. Use *soft* beancurd: its custard-like texture and mild flavour work with the sugar to neutralise the metallic edge of the spinach. The bean thread noodles give substance to this warming soup.

Serves 4

2 oz (50 g) bean thread (transparent) noodles
1½ lb (700 g) fresh spinach
8 oz (225 g) soft beancurd
2 pints (1.1 ltr) chicken or vegetable stock
2 tablespoons light soy sauce
3 tablespoons rice wine or dry sherry
2 teaspoons sugar
½ teaspoon salt

Soak the noodles in a large bowl of warm water for 15 minutes. When soft, drain them and discard the water. Cut the noodles into 3 inch (7.5 cm) lengths using scissors or a knife. Remove the stalks from the spinach and wash the leaves well. Gently cut the beancurd into 1 inch (2.5 cm) cubes.

Put the stock into a saucepan and bring to simmering point. Add the bean thread noodles and simmer for 2 minutes. Add the spinach and the rest of the ingredients except the beancurd. Simmer for 2 minutes, then gently put in the beancurd. Continue to simmer the soup for a further 2 minutes to heat the beancurd through. Serve at once.

TANGY TOMATO SOUP WITH LEMONGRASS
Photograph between pages 80 and 81

This Thai–Chinese recipe is so intertwined that it is difficult to differentiate the various contributors. The Thai cuisine specialises in hot, tangy, spicy soups that are refreshing and stimulating. The Chinese cuisine includes many soups that are as beautiful as they are flavoursome, providing the eggflower motif – attractive strands of lace-like white of egg. The lemongrass, refreshing and aromatic, is used in both cuisines. This impressive yet easy to make soup could be served at the grandest dinner. Alternatively, simply add blanched rice noodles to the soup and it becomes a meal in itself.

Serves 2 to 4

2 pints (1.1 ltr) chicken or vegetable stock
1 lb (450 g) fresh or tinned tomatoes
1 fresh lemongrass stalk or 1 tablespoon finely chopped lemon rind
1½ teaspoons salt
2 teaspoons sugar
1 tablespoon lemon juice
2 tablespoons finely chopped spring onions
1 small chilli, sliced
1 tablespoon finely chopped fresh coriander
1 egg white
2 teaspoons sesame oil

Garnish
coriander leaves

Put the stock in a saucepan and bring to simmering point. If using fresh tomatoes, peel, seed and cut the flesh into 1 inch (2.5 cm) cubes. If using tinned tomatoes, chop into small chunks. Peel the lemongrass stalk to the tender whitish centre and finely chop it.

Add the salt, sugar, lemon juice, spring onions, chilli and coriander to the simmering stock and stir to mix well. Add the tomatoes and simmer for 3 minutes. Lightly beat the egg white and combine with the sesame oil in a small bowl. Pour the egg white mixture into the soup in a very slow, thin stream. Using a chopstick or fork, pull the egg slowly into strands. (I have found that stirring the egg white in a figure-of-eight works quite well.) Garnish with the coriander leaves and serve.

SIZZLING RICE SOUP

This soup delights not only the eye, the nose and the palate, but the ear as well. I always enjoy making it because, as well as the dramatic sizzling, it is so full of flavour and easy to do. The ingredients are simple, requiring little preparation, much of which can be done ahead of time. Rice cakes are easy to make, once you have prepared them a few times. The key point to remember is that the oil used for deep-frying the pieces must be *very* hot to ensure that they become very crispy and not greasy – almost like dried popcorn. While the soup itself reheats well, the rice cake pieces must be deep-fried just before serving.

Serves 4

1 oz (25 g) Chinese dried mushrooms
½ oz (10 g) Chinese dried wood ears
2 pints (1.1 ltr) chicken or vegetable stock
1 lb (450 g) soft beancurd, cut into ½ inch (1 cm) cubes
4 tablespoons finely chopped spring onions
3 tablespoons rice wine or dry sherry
2 tablespoons light soy sauce
2 teaspoons chilli oil
½ teaspoon salt
Rice Cake (page 62)
1 pint (570 ml) oil, preferably groundnut, for deep-frying

Garnish
fresh coriander leaves

In separate bowls, soak the dried mushrooms and wood ears in warm water for 20 minutes. Drain them and squeeze out any excess liquid. Trim off the tough stalks and shred the mushroom caps and wood ears into 2 inch (5 cm) strips.

Bring the stock to simmering point in a large saucepan. Add the remaining soup ingredients, setting aside the rice cake and oil for deep-frying. Simmer for 20 minutes before transferring the soup to a large serving bowl.

Meanwhile, heat the oil in a large frying-pan or wok until it is nearly smoking. Drop in a grain of rice to test the heat – the rice should bubble all over and immediately come up to the surface.

Cut the rice cake into pieces and deep-fry for about 1–2 minutes until they puff up and brown slightly. Remove immediately with a slotted spoon and drain on kitchen paper. Quickly transfer the pieces to a platter and slide them into the soup. It should sizzle dramatically. Garnish with the fresh coriander leaves and serve at once.

RICE CAKE

Makes a 9 inch (23 cm) rice cake

8 oz (225 g) long-grain white rice
1 pint (570 ml) water
2 teaspoons oil, preferably groundnut

Wash the rice and put into a $9-9\frac{1}{2}$ inch (23–24 cm) wide, heavy saucepan with the water. Bring the water to the boil over high heat. Turn the heat down as low as possible, cover and cook the rice for about 45 minutes. The rice should form a heavy crust on the base of the pan. Remove all the loose surface rice, leaving the thick crust. (This loose rice can be used for making any of the fried rice recipes in Chapter 8.)

Dribble the oil evenly over the top of the rice cake and cook over a very low heat for 5 minutes. The cake should lift off easily at this point. If it is still sticky, add another teaspoon of oil and continue to cook until the whole cake comes loose. Put the cake onto a plate until required.

Once cooked, it can be left at room temperature for several days. Do *not* cover the rice cake, as moisture will form and make it soggy. Let the rice cake dry out. It is then ready to be cut into several pieces, deep-fried and put into the Sizzling Rice Soup (see previous recipe). As a simple snack, break it into chunks and eat hot with a sprinkling of salt.

JAPANESE SEAWEED SOUP

This light, rather austere soup is typical of Japanese cookery. Seaweed is high in protein and evokes the essence of the sea, and as nothing should mask this delicate rich flavour, the soup is kept very simple. The dried seaweed is well worth searching for. Once the stock is made and the seaweed soaked, the recipe can be quickly put together in a matter of minutes.

Serves 4

3 sheets 6 × 8 inches (15 × 20.5 cm) dried wakame seaweed
2 pints (1.1 ltr) dashi (page 16), or chicken or vegetable stock
rind of 1 lemon or lime, cut into thin matchsticks
½ teaspoon salt
2 tablespoons light soy sauce

Soak the seaweed for 20 minutes in warm water or until soft. Drain and cut it into thin shreds.

Bring the stock to simmering point in a large saucepan. Add the lemon rind, salt and light soy sauce and continue to simmer for another 2 minutes. Remove the soup from the heat and add the seaweed. Serve at once.

INDONESIAN CAULIFLOWER SOUP

Cauliflower is a delicately flavoured vegetable with a firm texture. In a soup such as this, it retains its pleasing characteristics while combining well with the distinctive flavours of coriander and cumin. The egg noodles add substance to the dish.

In its original Indonesian version, the soup is usually made with beef stock, but I prefer to use the lighter chicken or vegetable stock. Served with fresh bread (toasted perhaps) and a green salad, this hearty soup is a meal in itself.

Serves 2 to 4

1 lb (450 g) cauliflower
1 tablespoon oil, preferably groundnut
1 tablespoon finely chopped garlic
1 small onion, finely chopped
1½ teaspoons salt
¼ teaspoon freshly ground black pepper
1 teaspoon ground coriander
2 teaspoons ground cumin
2 pints (1.1 ltr) chicken or vegetable stock
4 oz (110 g) dried or fresh egg noodles

Garnish
1 tablespoon finely chopped fresh coriander

Cut the cauliflower into florets about 1–1½ inches (2.5–4 cm) wide.

Heat a wok or large frying-pan and add the oil. Put in the garlic, onion, $\frac{1}{2}$ teaspoon of the salt, pepper, coriander and cumin and stir-fry for about 2 minutes. Add the stock and cauliflower and simmer the mixture for 20 minutes or until the cauliflower is cooked.

Add the noodles to the simmering soup and cook for 8–10 minutes for dried noodles or 4–5 minutes for fresh noodles.

Add the remaining salt and give the soup a good stir. Transfer to a soup tureen and serve at once garnished with the coriander.

SWEETCORN AND GINGER SOUP

Sweetcorn soup with crab or chicken has become a very popular dish in many Chinese restaurants in the West. It is not truly Chinese but rather reflects a blend of Eastern and Western traditions. Here is my version of the soup, a lighter vegetarian one that contains the zest of fresh ginger to enliven it. I prefer to use fresh sweetcorn, as I find the starch used in the tinned variety tends to make the soup heavy. The milk in the recipe is definitely borrowed from the Western tradition; for a richer taste, use cream. This is an elegant starter for any dinner party.

Serves 4 to 6

$1\frac{1}{2}$ *lb (700 g) fresh sweetcorn on the cob, or 15 oz (425 g)*
  tinned sweetcorn kernels
1 egg, beaten
$\frac{1}{2}$ *teaspoon sesame oil*
1 tablespoon oil, preferably groundnut
1 tablespoon finely chopped fresh ginger
2 pints (1.1 ltr) chicken or vegetable stock
2 tablespoons rice wine or dry sherry
5 fl oz (150 ml) milk
2 teaspoons salt
$\frac{1}{2}$ *teaspoon freshly ground white pepper*
1 tablespoon sugar

Garnish
1 tablespoon finely chopped spring onions

If you are using fresh sweetcorn, remove the kernels with a sharp knife or cleaver – you should end up with about 15 oz (425 g). Mix the egg and sesame oil together in a small bowl and set aside.

Heat a large saucepan until moderately hot. Add the oil and ginger and stir-fry for 30 seconds. Add the rest of the ingredients, except the corn, egg mixture and spring onions. Bring the mixture to the boil and add the corn. Simmer for 15 minutes, uncovered, and then allow it to cool slightly.

Purée the soup in a blender or food mill until light and creamy. Return the soup to the pan and bring to a slow simmer. Add the egg mixture, stirring all the time. For serving, transfer the soup to a tureen or individual bowls and garnish with the spring onions.

SPINACH AND EGG-RIBBON SOUP
Photograph between pages 80 and 81

When a soup appears as beautiful as it tastes, it is safe to assume a Japanese influence, as with this light soup. Try to make it with the Japanese dashi (page 16), which is essential for the authentic flavour; but if it is not available, a good chicken or vegetable stock produces a fine soup. The attractive 'egg ribbons' are made by pulling or stretching the egg strands with a fork or chopsticks as you pour them slowly into the soup.

Serves 4

4 oz (110 g) fresh spinach
2 pints (1.1 ltr) dashi (page 16), or chicken or vegetable stock
2 eggs, beaten
1 teaspoon fresh ginger juice (page 17)
1 teaspoon salt
1 tablespoon sake, rice wine or dry sherry
1 teaspoon cornflour mixed with 1 teaspoon water

Remove the stalks from the spinach and wash the leaves well. Blanch them for a few seconds in a pan of boiling water until they are just wilted. Freshen the leaves in cold water to prevent further cooking.

Put the stock into a saucepan and bring to simmering point. Lightly beat the eggs and combine them with the ginger juice. Add the salt, sake and blended cornflour to the simmering stock, and stir to mix well. Pour in the egg mixture in a very slow, thin stream. Using a chopstick or fork, pull the egg slowly into strands. Drain the spinach and add to the hot soup before serving.

STEAMED VEGETABLE SOUP

This is one of my favourite soups. In China, it is called 'double-boiled' or 'double-steamed', the name deriving from the cooking technique used. The prepared ingredients are put in a casserole containing a boiling rich stock; then the casserole is sealed and placed in a steamer – a double cooking process that creates a flavourful soup. It is popular among all Chinese, and in Hong Kong it is made from various ingredients, such as shark fins, pigeons, bird's nests, chicken and, as in this recipe, vegetables. Because vegetables cook quickly, this takes little more than half an hour to cook to full flavour and the result is a clear soup, rather like a rich consommé. It makes a splendid first course for dinner parties or can be served as part of a family meal.

Serves 4 to 6

1 oz (25 g) Chinese dried mushrooms
4 oz (110 g) Chinese white radish (mooli)
4 oz (110 g) fresh or tinned waterchestnuts
2 eggs, beaten
1 teaspoon salt
1 teaspoon sesame oil
1 tablespoon oil, preferably groundnut
2 pints (1.1 ltr) chicken or vegetable stock

Garnish
watercress leaves

Soak the dried mushrooms in warm water for 20 minutes until they are soft. Squeeze the excess liquid from the mushrooms and remove and discard the stalks. Leave the caps whole.

Peel and cut the Chinese radish into 3 inch (7.5 cm) long pieces. If you are using fresh waterchestnuts, peel them; if you are using tinned waterchestnuts, drain well and rinse in cold water. Thinly slice the waterchestnuts. Beat the eggs, $\frac{1}{2}$ teaspoon of the salt and the sesame oil together in a small bowl.

Heat a wok or frying-pan until hot and add the oil. Pour in the egg mixture and cook until it sets. Remove the omelette and leave to cool. Cut it into $\frac{1}{2}$ inch (1 cm) shreds.

Set a rack into a wok or deep pan. Fill with $2\frac{1}{2}$ inches (6 cm) water and bring it to the boil. Bring the stock to the boil in another large pan and then pour the stock into a heatproof glass or china casserole. Add the radish, waterchestnuts, egg shreds, mushrooms and remaining salt to the stock. Cover and put the casserole on the rack, then cover the wok or deep pan tightly with a lid or foil. You now have a casserole within a steamer, hence the name 'double-boil'. Reduce the heat and steam gently for 35 minutes or until the radish is cooked. Replenish the hot water from time to time. An alternative method is to simply simmer the soup very slowly in a conventional pan, but the resulting taste will be quite different.

When the soup is cooked, it can be served immediately or cooled and stored in the refrigerator or freezer to be reheated when required. Garnish the soup with the watercress just before serving.

FIERY SICHUAN SOUP

One of the great virtues of Chinese and most oriental cookery is their adaptability when confronted with new influences. This hot and spicy soup, now so popular in the West, is traditionally made with pork but, when dried mushrooms and cloud ears (black fungus) are substituted, the soup retains its excellent qualities and remains a substantial and nutritious meal. Do try to obtain the dried mushrooms and cloud ears – their textures are quite special.

Serves 4

2 oz (50 g) bean thread (transparent) noodles
½ oz (10 g) Chinese dried mushrooms
½ oz (10 g) Chinese dried cloud ears (black fungus)
4 oz (110 g) bamboo shoots, shredded
1 egg, beaten
2 teaspoons sesame oil
2 pints (1.1 ltr) chicken or vegetable stock
1 tablespoon finely chopped fresh ginger
2 tablespoons tomato purée
1 tablespoon light soy sauce
2 tablespoons dark soy sauce
2 teaspoons chilli oil
1 tablespoon black rice vinegar or cider vinegar
2 teaspoons freshly ground black pepper

Garnish
3 tablespoons finely chopped spring onions

Soak the noodles in a large bowl of warm water for 15 minutes. When they are soft, drain and discard the water. Cut the noodles into 3 inch (7.5 cm) lengths, using scissors or a knife.

Soak the dried mushrooms and cloud ears in separate bowls of warm water for 20 minutes until soft. Squeeze the excess liquid from the mushrooms and remove and discard the stalks. Rinse the cloud ears in cold water, drain well and leave whole. Shred the mushroom caps finely. Finely shred the bamboo shoots. Beat the eggs and sesame oil together in a small bowl.

Bring the stock to simmering point in a large pan. Add the mushrooms, cloud ears, bamboo shoots, noodles and the rest of the ingredients, except the egg mixture and spring onions. Simmer for 5 minutes.

Finally, pour the beaten egg mixture into the soup in a steady stream. Pull the egg into strands with a fork or chopsticks. Garnish with the spring onions and pour the soup into a large tureen or individual bowls. Serve at once.

FRAGRANT NOODLE SOUP

Egg noodles are a simple and comforting food – plain, homely, nutritious and satisfying. Combined with soup, their virtues are magnified, and when we add a touch of Southeast Asian zest – lime juice and fish sauce – the result is a wholesome soup that can serve as a light lunch for two or as a starter for any meal.

Serves 2 to 4

8 oz (225 g) fresh or dried egg noodles
2 pints (1.1 ltr) chicken or vegetable stock
2 tablespoons finely chopped spring onions
1 tablespoon finely chopped fresh coriander
4 oz (110 g) celery, finely chopped
2 teaspoons sesame oil
1 tablespoon chilli oil
1 tablespoon fish sauce
1 tablespoon lime juice
1 tablespoon light soy sauce
2 teaspoons sugar

If you are using fresh noodles, blanch them for 3–5 minutes in a large pan of boiling water, then immerse in cold water. If you are using dried noodles, cook in boiling water for 4–5 minutes. Drain the noodles, cool in cold water until required.

Put the stock into a pan and bring to simmering point. Add the rest of the ingredients and simmer for 5 minutes. Drain the noodles and add them to the soup. Bring the soup back to simmering point and serve at once.

SOUTHEAST ASIAN VEGETABLE SOUP
Photograph between pages 80 and 81

I have savoured the fragrance and taste of curry ever since I was a small child. It was quite a surprise to me when I discovered that curry is based on Indian and not Chinese inventiveness. Here is a vegetable soup which is raised by its seasonings above the ordinary into something rather special; it is the curry which dominates (without suffocating) the other flavours.

Serves 4 to 6

4 oz (110 g) carrots
4 oz (110 g) courgettes
4 oz (110 g) potatoes
4 oz (110 g) Chinese long beans, runner or French beans, trimmed
4 oz (110 g) Chinese leaves
2 tablespoons oil, preferably groundnut
2 tablespoons finely chopped garlic
2 tablespoons finely chopped fresh lemongrass
2 oz (50 g) onions, finely chopped
2 teaspoons turmeric
2 tablespoons curry paste
1½ pints (900 ml) chicken or vegetable stock
15 fl oz (400 ml) fresh or tinned coconut milk (page 14)
1 tablespoon salt

Peel and cut the carrots into 1 inch (2.5 cm) rounds. Slice the courgettes into rounds ¼ inch (0.5 cm) thick, or roll cut them (see page 32). Peel and cut the potatoes into 1 inch (2.5 cm) cubes. Trim and cut the beans into 3 inch (7.5 cm) lengths. Cut the Chinese leaves into 1 inch (2.5 cm) pieces.

Heat the oil in a large saucepan until hot. Add the garlic, lemongrass and onions and cook for about 2 minutes. Stir in the turmeric and curry paste and continue to cook for another 2 minutes. Add the vegetables, stock, coconut milk and salt. Simmer for 8 minutes or until the vegetables are cooked through.

CREAMY AUBERGINE AND TOMATO SOUP

This soup is of Indonesian origin. Aubergines are a popular vegetable throughout Southeast Asia. 'Eggplant', as they are called in the USA, derive from the white-skinned egg-shaped variety common in India. In this recipe, tomatoes (a relatively recent addition) are combined with coconut milk (a traditional ingredient) in a vegetable or chicken stock to create a nutritious soup that is hearty without being heavy.

Serves 4 to 6

12 oz (350 g) aubergine
8 oz (225 g) fresh or tinned tomatoes
4 oz (110 g) onion
1 fresh chilli, seeded
1½ pints (900 ml) chicken or vegetable stock
15 fl oz (400 ml) fresh or tinned coconut milk (page 14)
2 tablespoons oil, preferably groundnut
2 tablespoons finely chopped garlic
2 teaspoons sugar
2 teaspoons salt or to taste
½ teaspoon freshly ground white pepper

Peel and cut the aubergine into ½ inch (1 cm) cubes. If you are using fresh tomatoes, peel, seed and cut them into 1 inch (2.5 cm) cubes. If you are using tinned tomatoes, cut them into small chunks. Finely chop the onion and chilli.

Bring the stock and coconut milk to simmering point in a large saucepan. While simmering, heat a wok or large frying-pan and add the oil. When hot, put in the onion, garlic, chilli and aubergine and stir-fry over high heat for about 4 minutes until nicely browned. Drain on kitchen paper, then add to the soup. Add the rest of the ingredients and simmer for 5 minutes.

THREE

COLD DISHES & SALADS

Many oriental dishes contain spices and flavourings that make them delicious, whether they are served hot or cold. Coldness tends to blunt the taste of spices and seasonings, hence you can use more of them in cold dishes. In China, there is a lively tradition of serving intricately designed cold food platters at banquets and other special occasions. This is no accident. When food is to be served cold, it is naturally prepared well ahead of time, making it perfect for large gatherings and buffets and, in our day, for picnics. Cold dishes also make warm weather dining more agreeable and pleasant.

Raw vegetable salads are almost unknown in Asia. There, food is always cooked at least a little before it is deemed ready for a sauce or dressing. There are several reasons for this, most notably reasons of hygiene. Brief cooking destroys any bacteria or tiny insects in the vegetables that could be harmful. In traditional societies without a supply of clean water, the eating of raw foods is often unwise; warm weather with no refrigeration contributes to the rapid growth of bacteria, also a potential danger. Quick cooking renders food both safe and more easily digestible.

You will find many of these dishes blend well with your everyday meals. For example, the Peppery Aubergines make a delicious family starter, or serve Asparagus with Tangy Mustard Dressing at a dinner party.

PEPPERY AUBERGINES

India and the Far East consume the greatest quantities of aubergines. This is to be expected as, although this splendid vegetable is not cultivated in warm climates throughout the world, its homeland is India. It has been a traditional food in Eastern cookery for many centuries. This recipe was inspired by my good friend Hwang San in his delightful Hunan-style restaurant, Dong Ting, in Houston, Texas. He steams the aubergines, but I find roasting them just as easy with the same results. Aubergines have a very spongy texture and can absorb a great deal of oil when they are fried or even stir-fried.

This dish works well as a starter. The cooked aubergine is not too filling and the peppercorn sauce stimulates the palate. Because this dish may be made well ahead of time, it is quite practical for entertaining. It is an excellent picnic dish too.

Serves 4

1 lb (450 g) aubergines

Sauce
1 ½ teaspoons Sichuan peppercorns, roasted and ground (page 24)
1 ½ teaspoons salt
1 teaspoon sugar
2 tablespoons sesame oil
6 tablespoons finely chopped spring onion tops
2 teaspoons finely chopped fresh coriander
1 tablespoon Chinese white rice vinegar or cider vinegar

Preheat the oven to Gas Mark 6, 400°F (200°C). If you are using Chinese aubergines, roast for 20 minutes; if you are using the large aubergines, roast for about 30–40 minutes or until they are soft to the touch and cooked through. Allow the aubergines to cool, then peel them. Shred or cut the aubergine flesh into strips.

Arrange the aubergine on a platter. Combine the sauce ingredients, pour over the aubergine and serve at once.

HOT AND SOUR CUCUMBER SALAD

In Thailand, the cucumbers are shorter and thicker than the Western variety. They also fairly bursting with seeds. But no matter, for whatever type we use, the cucumber's mild flavour and juicy crunchiness comes through. In this recipe, the cucumbers are marinated in a piquant vinegary dressing, making them an ideal accompaniment to any fried or grilled dishes. They may also be served as a salad in their own right. By all means experiment: you may find you enjoy an even spicier version. Just add more chillies and garlic.

Serves 4

1 lb (450 g) cucumbers
2 fl oz (50 ml) white rice or cider vinegar
1 tablespoon sugar
1 teaspoon salt
½ oz (10 g) fresh red chilli, finely sliced
1 teaspoon finely chopped garlic

Slice the cucumbers in half lengthways and, using a teaspoon, remove the seeds. Cut the cucumber halves into $3 \times \frac{1}{2}$ inch (7.5 × 1 cm) pieces.

Combine the cucumber pieces with the rest of the ingredients in a bowl and leave to stand for at least 4 hours or more in the refrigerator, stirring from time to time. When you are ready to serve, drain the cucumber thoroughly.

SESAME-DRESSED SPINACH SALAD

Spinach is used extensively in Japanese, Chinese and Indonesian cooking. I have often enjoyed this spinach salad in Japanese restaurants in Southeast Asia, and I was pleased to learn how simple it is to make. In Japan, spinach is picked when it is still quite a small plant; this assures a sweet and tender leaf. The essential technique is to blanch the spinach quickly, plunge it into cold water (to stop the cooking and to preserve the deep colour) and to squeeze out all excess liquid. The spinach is then ready to absorb the flavours of the marinade.

Serves 2 to 4

$1\frac{1}{2}$ *lb (700 g) fresh spinach*
1 teaspoon toasted sesame seeds (page 23)

Dressing
$\frac{1}{2}$ *teaspoon salt*
$1\frac{1}{2}$ *tablespoons light soy sauce*
2 teaspoons sugar
2 teaspoons Chinese white rice vinegar or cider vinegar
1 tablespoon oil, preferably groundnut

Wash the spinach thoroughly and remove the stalks. Blanch the leaves in a saucepan of boiling salted water for about 30 seconds. Drain and immerse the leaves in cold water. Drain in a colander. Put the spinach inside a clean linen tea towel and squeeze out all the excess liquid.

Combine all the dressing ingredients in a small bowl and mix thoroughly. Combine the spinach and dressing and leave the salad to marinate in the dressing for at least $1\frac{1}{2}$ hours before serving, or refrigerate and serve within 3 hours. Sprinkle the toasted sesame seeds on top just before serving.

GREEN AND WHITE JADE SALAD
Photograph between pages 80 and 81

This colourful broccoli and cauliflower salad makes a fine starter or picnic dish. The well-flavoured dressing is equally delicious with other vegetable combinations, such as carrots and Brussels sprouts.

Serves 2 to 4

8 oz (225 g) broccoli
8 oz (225 g) cauliflower

Dressing
2 tablespoons sesame paste or peanut butter
1 tablespoon Chinese white rice vinegar or cider vinegar
1 teaspoon chilli oil
1 teaspoon sesame oil
1 tablespoon light soy sauce
1 teaspoon salt
2 teaspoons sugar

Cut off the broccoli heads and break them into small florets. Peel the broccoli stalks if necessary and slice. Cut the cauliflower into small florets, about $1-1\frac{1}{2}$ inches (2.5–3.5 cm) wide. Blanch the broccoli heads, stalks and cauliflower in a large saucepan of boiling salted water for 4 minutes. Plunge them into cold water, then drain. Dry the broccoli and cauliflower in a colander or salad spinner and arrange on a platter.

Mix the dressing ingredients together in a bowl or a blender. (This can be done in advance and kept refrigerated as the sauce should be cold.) Pour the dressing over the vegetables and serve.

EAST–WEST SHREDDED SALAD
Photograph between pages 80 and 81

Raw or almost raw vegetables are enjoyed in most countries, both East and West, but not in China where they are usually at least stir-fried, blanched or pickled. I enjoy raw vegetables, thus showing my Western culinary influences, but I understand the Chinese preference also. Hence, this East–West compromise: delicious, fresh raw vegetables covered with a heated zesty Chinese-inspired sauce that coats the salad. The result pleases both eye and palate, and creates a refreshing salad for any meal.

Serves 2 to 4

4 oz (110 g) carrots
1 oz (25 g) fresh chillies (optional)
4 spring onions
8 oz (225 g) iceberg lettuce
2 oz (50 g) bean sprouts

Dressing
1 tablespoon finely chopped fresh ginger
2 dried chillies, chopped
3 tablespoons finely chopped spring onions
½ teaspoon Sichuan peppercorns, roasted and ground (page 24)
1 tablespoon light soy sauce
1 tablespoon Chinese white rice vinegar or cider vinegar
2 tablespoons oil, preferably groundnut
2 teaspoons sesame oil

Peel and cut the carrots into 2 inch (5 cm) fine shreds. Cut the chillies, spring onions and lettuce into 2 inch (5 cm) fine shreds. In a large bowl, mix all the vegetables together.

Combine all the dressing ingredients, except the oils, in a heat-proof bowl. Heat the oils in a small saucepan or wok until almost smoking. Pour the hot oils over the dressing ingredients and allow to cool for 5 minutes. Pour the dressing over the vegetables and toss thoroughly. Serve at once.

SPINACH IN OYSTER SAUCE

Spinach is a nutritious vegetable with a fine flavour. The trend throughout the West is of consuming more and more fresh spinach instead of tinned or frozen, and raw spinach leaves are increasingly used in salad. This recipe is based on a traditional southern Chinese method but, instead of serving the cooked spinach warm, I serve it cold. In the area around Canton there is a variety called water spinach, which has a milder taste and which, when cooked, presents a pleasing contrast between the crunchy stalk and soft leaves. It may sometimes be found in Chinese grocers and I encourage you to look for it to try, but ordinary fresh spinach will do very well.

Serves 2 to 4

$1\frac{1}{2}$ *lb (700 g) fresh spinach*

Sauce
$1\frac{1}{2}$ *tablespoons oyster sauce*
2 teaspoons sesame oil
2 teaspoons sugar

Remove the stalks from the spinach and wash the leaves well.
Blanch the leaves for a few seconds in a saucepan of boiling water
until just wilted. Remove and freshen them in cold water to prevent
further cooking. Drain the leaves in a colander, then place on a
linen tea towel and squeeze out all the excess liquid. Arrange on a
serving dish.

Mix the sauce ingredients together and pour over the spinach.
This dish can remain at room temperature until ready to serve.

CHINESE AUBERGINE SALAD

Fish sauce makes a piquant dressing for this aubergine salad.
Roasting the aubergines preserves their moist, sweet flavour.
Quickly made, this dish can be served warm or cold.

Serves 4

1 lb (450 g) aubergines

Dressing
2 tablespoons finely chopped spring onions
2 teaspoons chilli oil
2 teaspoons fish sauce
1 tablespoon light soy sauce
1 teaspoon finely chopped garlic

Preheat the oven to Gas Mark 6, 400°F (200°C). If you are using
Chinese aubergines, roast for 20 minutes; if you are using the
large aubergines, roast for about 30–40 minutes or until they are
soft and cooked through. Allow to cool, then peel. Cut the aubergine flesh into strips.

Arrange the aubergine on a platter. Combine the dressing
ingredients and pour over the aubergine. Serve the salad immediately or refrigerate and serve the next day.

COLD GREEN BEAN SALAD

Simplicity itself, this recipe takes a favourite vegetable and gives it a touch of Southeast Asian zest. The fish sauce is commonly used in many parts of Southeast Asia and, when combined with other spices, will enliven any dish. Serve these beans either as a salad or as a side vegetable dish. They may be prepared well ahead of time.

Serves 2 to 4

8 oz (225 g) Chinese long beans, runner or French beans, trimmed
1 tablespoon oil, preferably groundnut
1 small onion, finely chopped

Dressing
1 tablespoon fish sauce
2 teaspoons toasted sesame seeds (page 23)
2 tablespoons lemon juice
2 teaspoons sesame oil
1 teaspoon salt
2 teaspoons chilli oil

If you are using Chinese long beans or runner beans, cut them into 3 inch (7.5 cm) lengths. If you are using French beans, leave whole. Blanch the beans in a large saucepan of boiling salted water for 2 minutes. Immerse them in cold water, drain thoroughly and set aside.

Heat a wok or frying-pan and add the oil. When moderately hot, add the onion and stir-fry for 2 minutes, then allow to cool. Add to the beans.

Combine all the dressing ingredients and toss with the beans and onion. Serve the salad immediately or refrigerate and serve the next day.

BEAN SPROUT SALAD

Photograph opposite page 144

Bean sprouts have been enjoyed in China and Southeast Asia for centuries but have only recently been introduced to the West. They are essentially a transitional food, as it were, midway between the seed or bean from which they spring and the vegetable they will become. They have significant nutritional value, a nutty flavour and crisp texture as well. Mung beans and soya beans are the favoured sprouts among the Chinese, who love them cooked but never in raw form. Lightly blanched, as in this recipe, the sprouts lose their raw taste but retain their crispness and flavour. This salad is easily made and can be prepared hours in advance. Refreshing and spicy, it goes well with grilled meats.

Serves 4

1 lb (450 g) fresh bean sprouts
1 fresh red chilli, seeded and finely shredded

Dressing
$1\frac{1}{2}$ tablespoons light soy sauce
1 teaspoon oil, preferably groundnut
2 teaspoons sesame oil
1 teaspoon chilli oil
1 teaspoon finely chopped garlic
2 tablespoons finely chopped spring onions
$\frac{1}{2}$ teaspoon sugar
$\frac{1}{2}$ teaspoon salt
$\frac{1}{4}$ teaspoon freshly ground white pepper

Trim and discard both ends of the bean sprouts. Blanch the bean sprouts in a large saucepan of boiling water for 1 minute. Drain in a colander, immerse them in cold water, then drain again.

Combine the dressing ingredients in a small bowl. Mix the dressing together with the bean sprouts and chilli.

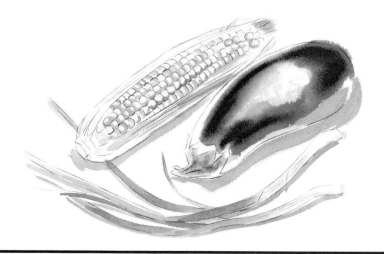

ASPARAGUS WITH TANGY MUSTARD DRESSING
Photograph opposite page 144

Asparagus is a relative newcomer to the cast of vegetables in oriental cuisine, but there is no doubt it has won a permanent starring role in the repertory. Its popularity is based on contrasts: properly cooked, it has a firm but soft texture, a delicate yet earthy assertive flavour – and a brilliant colour. In this Japanese-style recipe, the asparagus is simply cooked by quickly blanching, the briefest processing possible. The mustard-ginger dressing only highlights and never intrudes upon the taste of the asparagus. Since asparagus is relatively expensive, indulge yourself and savour this recipe when it is in season. Serve it as a starter or side dish for a special meal.

Serves 2 to 4

1 lb (450 g) fresh asparagus

Dressing
1 teaspoon dried mustard
1 teaspoon hot water
1 egg yolk
1 tablespoon dark soy sauce
1 teaspoon finely chopped fresh ginger
$\frac{1}{4}$ teaspoon salt

Break off the woody ends of the asparagus and cut the stalks into 3 inch (7.5 cm) diagonal pieces. Blanch the asparagus in a large saucepan of boiling salted water for 2 minutes. Plunge them into cold water, then drain in a colander. Pat dry with kitchen paper.

In a small bowl, mix the mustard and hot water together and stir until a thick paste. Add the rest of the dressing ingredients and mix well.

Arrange the asparagus on a serving platter and pour the dressing over. Serve immediately or within 3 hours.

Opposite: *Crispy Vegetarian Wuntuns (page 49) and Crispy Cabbage with Sugar Walnuts (page 42)*
Overleaf: *Spinach and Egg-Ribbon Soup (page 65), Tangy Tomato Soup with Lemongrass (page 60) and Southeast Asian Vegetable Soup (page 69); Green and White Jade Salad (page 75) and East–West Shredded Salad (page 75)*

CRISPY NOODLE SALAD

I first enjoyed this salad, called Mee Krob, in a rather unpretentious restaurant in Bangkok. There are a number of different variations on the crispy noodle salad theme, with many people preferring a sweet and sour salad. At home, I set out to recreate the combination of textures, flavours and colours that had most impressed me in Thailand, and this recipe is my favourite – a beautifully arranged salad platter that is dressed and tossed at the last minute. Such a salad is ideal as a starter for any meal.

Serves 4

10 fl oz (300 ml) oil, preferably groundnut, for deep-frying
4 oz (110 g) rice noodles, rice vermicelli or rice sticks

Sauce

2 cloves garlic, crushed
2 tablespoons finely chopped shallots
3 tablespoons fish sauce
1 tablespoon sugar
2 tablespoons Chinese white vinegar or cider vinegar

Garnish

4 oz (110 g) beancurd, cut into small dice
4 oz (110 g) bean sprouts
3 spring onions, shredded
1 fresh chilli, shredded
fresh coriander sprigs

Heat the oil in a deep-fat fryer or wok until moderately hot. Deep-fry the noodles until crispy and puffed up. Remove from the oil with a slotted spoon and drain on kitchen paper. You may have to do this in several batches. (Leave the oil in the deep-fat fryer or wok as you will need it for the beancurd.)

Cut the beancurd into ½ inch (1 cm) cubes. Reheat the oil until very hot and deep-fry the beancurd cubes until golden. Remove with a slotted spoon and drain on kitchen paper.

Combine the sauce ingredients in a small bowl and mix well.

Place the crispy noodles on a serving platter and garnish attractively with the beancurd, bean sprouts, spring onions, chilli and coriander. Pour the dressing over the salad just before serving and mix well.

Opposite: *Grilled Beancurd Shish Kebabs (page 116) and Red-Cooked Beancurd (page 125)*

FOUR

VEGETABLE DISHES

Vegetables are important in any cuisine that is nutritious, flavourful and colourful. In the Cantonese cuisine of south China, considered among the most nutritious in the world, more vegetables of diverse texture, shape, size and colour are used than in almost any other culinary tradition. My mother, who is of Cantonese origin, consequently relied heavily on vegetables in our home cooking. She used traditional Chinese vegetables whenever they were available, but she reached out to harvest the Western cornucopia as well. In Chinese cookery, technique is more important even than the ingredients. My mother took standard European vegetables and prepared them so well that, unlike my Western schoolmates, I loved to eat them. As my mother cooked them, the vegetables retained their fresh flavours, textures, nutritious vitamins and colours.

Many vegetables have delicate textures; most have only subtle flavours. How does one cook them and yet preserve their qualities? Well, practice makes perfect, especially to avoid overcooking. With vegetables, you need to nibble, taste, nibble, taste as you cook. Below are a few guidelines I have found helpful:

■ If vegetables in the raw state are soft, leafy, delicate and full of moisture, like spinach, Chinese greens and lettuce, they need very little cooking. A simple blanching or quick stir-frying in a little oil with intense heat will cook them to perfection. Stir-frying at high heat seals in their moisture and flavours; low heat will steam them and draw out moisture, leaving them dry with an overcooked taste and appearance. If you blanch these vegetables, plunge them immediately afterwards into cold water to stop them from cooking; this also sets and preserves their vivid colours.

■ Some vegetables are what I call 'in-between'. That is, they are not soft, like spinach, nor are they firm and crunchy like carrots. They usually contain some moisture but are crisp and do need some cooking. I have in mind vegetables such as courgettes, mange-tout, red and green peppers and cucumbers. 'Salting' is usually a good technique for preparing courgettes and cucumbers for cooking. This method draws out some of the liquid while preserving their textures and flavours. Cook these vegetables a little longer than you would the more tender, leafy ones.

■ Then there are the 'hard' vegetables, such as carrots, Chinese white radish (mooli), broccoli, cauliflower and Brussels sprouts. These firm-textured vegetables usually require two separate cooking procedures – blanching to soften them and then stir-frying to cook them sufficiently and infuse them with additional flavours.

Alternatively, they can be cooked in a larger amount of liquid.

■ Not all vegetables are meant to be cooked 'just to the point'. Aubergines, bitter melon and Chinese leaves profit from more extensive cooking. Some release additional liquid or bitter juices in the cooking process.

■ If you are cooking a multi-vegetable dish or combining vegetables with other foods such as meat, fish or poultry, you can cook the different vegetables separately and *then* combine everything at the last moment. The result will be perfectly cooked every time because every element of the dish will have had its own correct cooking time.

■ Finally, a great deal of vegetable cookery involves common sense and experience. Don't worry, and trust your own judgement. If you make a mistake, it will be a valuable lesson for your next attempt.

In this book, I have included vegetable recipes from China, Japan, Korea and elsewhere in Southeast Asia. The vegetables, spices and seasonings have an oriental flavour that complements European foods. Experiment with them and include them in your everyday cookery. Some recipes include more exotic vegetables for those who are more adventurous, but most involve vegetables you can easily buy at your supermarket. Always insist on the best and freshest vegetables. Below is a list of vegetables which may not all be familiar to you.

AUBERGINES

Also known as eggplant, these smooth purple-skinned vegetables range in size from the huge fat ones which are easy to find in all greengrocers to the small thin variety which the Chinese prefer because they have a more delicate flavour.

The Chinese do not normally peel aubergines, since the skin preserves their texture, shape and taste. Large aubergines should be cut according to the recipe, sprinkled with a little salt and left to stand for 20 minutes. They should then be rinsed and any liquid blotted dry with kitchen paper. This process extracts excess moisture and bitter juices from the vegetable before it is cooked.

BEAN SPROUTS

Bean sprouts are now widely available in greengrocers, supermarkets and Chinese grocers. They are the sprouts of the green mung bean, although some Chinese grocers also stock yellow soya bean sprouts which are much larger. Bean sprouts should always be very fresh and crunchy. They will keep for several days wrapped in a plastic bag and stored in the vegetable compartment of a refrigerator. Never use tinned bean sprouts, as these have been pre-cooked and are soggy and tasteless.

To grow bean sprouts

It is very easy to grow your own bean sprouts. Dried mung beans (sometimes spelt moong) are obtainable from supermarkets, oriental grocers and health food shops. You will need to obtain or devise a perforated flat surface. An old tin plate or thin metal pan punched with holes, or a bamboo steamer, are all ideal. You will also need 2 pieces of muslin and 1 oz (25 g) dried green mung beans.

Wash the beans several times in water, then leave them to soak in lukewarm water for 8 hours or overnight. Once soaking is complete, rinse the beans again under warm running water until the water runs clear. Dampen the muslin and spread one piece over the tin lid, pan or steamer. Spread the beans over the cloth and sprinkle them with more lukewarm water. Cover the beans with the second piece of muslin and then put them in a warm, dark place. Keep them moist by sprinkling with water several times over the next few days. In 3 days you should have white crisp sprouts.

BITTER MELON

Used as a vegetable, bitter melon has a strong flavour worthy of its name. The greener the melon, the more bitter its taste, so many cooks look for the milder yellow-green skinned melon. To use, cut in half, seed and discard the interior membrane. To lessen the bitter taste, either blanch or salt according to the instructions in the recipe.

CHINESE BROCCOLI

Chinese broccoli or gai lan (*Brassica oleracea capitata*) does not taste like European broccoli (calabrese). It is very crunchy, slightly bitter and resembles Swiss chard in flavour. It has deep olive green leaves and sometimes has white flowers. Chinese broccoli is usually only available at Chinese grocers. If you can find it, look for firm stalks and leaves which look fresh and green. It is prepared in exactly the same way as broccoli, and should be stored in a plastic bag in the vegetable compartment of the refrigerator where it will keep for several days. If you cannot find Chinese broccoli, substitute ordinary broccoli instead.

CHINESE CHIVES

Chinese chives are related to common chives, but their taste is much stronger and garlic-like, and their flowers can be used as well as the blades. Chinese chives can be found in Chinese markets but are also very easy to grow in home herb gardens. Look for wide flat blades and sprays of white, star-shaped flowers. They can be substituted for ordinary chives, but adjust the quantity to allow for their stronger flavour. Rinse and dry the chives, store them in a plastic bag in the refrigerator and use as soon as possible.

CHINESE FLOWERING CABBAGE

Chinese flowering cabbage (*Brassica rapa*) is usually known by its more familiar Cantonese name, choi sam. It has yellowish green leaves and may have small yellow flowers which are eaten along with the leaves and stalks. It is obtainable from Chinese grocers and is delicious stir-fried.

CHINESE GREENS

Chinese greens (*Brassica chinensis*) is an attractive vegetable with a long, smooth, milky-white stalk and large, crinkly, dark green leaves. It is similar to Swiss chard, and has been grown for centuries in China, where it is known as bok choi. In the West, it is sometimes called Chinese white cabbage or Chinese chard, and it has a light fresh taste and requires little cooking. It is usually available from Chinese grocers. Swiss chard or spinach can be substituted if you cannot obtain Chinese greens.

CHINESE LEAVES

Chinese leaves (*Brassica pekinensis*) look rather like a large, tightly packed cos lettuce with firm, pale green, crinkled leaves. It is sometimes known as Chinese or Peking cabbage, and is widely available in greengrocers, supermarkets and Chinese grocers. It is a delicious crunchy vegetable with a mild but distinctive taste. If you cannot find it, use English white cabbage instead.

CHINESE LONG BEANS

Also known as yard-long beans. Chinese long beans (*Vigna sesquipedalis*) can grow to about 3 feet (1 metre) in length. Although runner beans and French beans can be substituted for the long beans, they are not related, the long beans having originated in Asia. Buy beans with fresh bright green texture and no dark marks.

You will usually find beans sold in looped bunches. Store the beans in a plastic bag in the refrigerator and use within 4 days.

CHINESE WHITE RADISH (MOOLI)

Chinese white radish is known better in this country as mooli. It is long and white and rather like a carrot in shape but usually very much larger. A winter radish or root, it can withstand long cooking without disintegrating, so it absorbs the flavour of a sauce yet retains its distinctive radish taste and texture. It must be peeled before use. Chinese white radish can be bought in many supermarkets and greengrocers (under the name mooli), and in oriental and Chinese grocers. They should be firm, heavy and unblemished, slightly translucent inside and not tough and fibrous. Store in a plastic bag in the vegetable compartment of the refrigerator where they will keep for over a week. If you cannot find white radish, use turnips instead.

MANGE-TOUT

These tender flat green pods combine a crisp texture with a sweet, fresh flavour. Mange-tout are delicious whether simply stir-fried with a little oil and salt, or combined with other ingredients. Shredded they add a crisp texture and sweet taste to stuffings and other dishes. They produce a unique crunchy salad when blanched and tossed in a dressing. Before cooking, the ends should be trimmed. Mange-tout are available from greengrocers and supermarkets. Look for pods that are firm with very small peas, which means they will be tender and young. They keep for at least a week in the vegetable compartment of the refrigerator.

SHALLOTS

Shallots are mild-flavoured members of the onion family. They are small – about the size of pickling onions – with copper-red skins and a distinctive onion taste. However, they are not as strong or overpowering as ordinary onions. I think they are an excellent substitute for Chinese onions, which are unobtainable in the West. They are expensive, but a few go a long way. Buy them at good greengrocers, supermarkets and delicatessens. Keep them in a cool, dry place (but not the refrigerator) and peel them as you would an onion. If you cannot find shallots, use pickling onions or spring onions.

SPINACH

European varieties of spinach are quite different from those used in China, although they make satisfactory substitutes for the Asian variety. Spinach is most commonly stir-fried, so frozen spinach is obviously unsuitable. Chinese water spinach (*Ipomoea aquatica*) is available in some greengrocers and in Chinese grocers. It has hollow stalks and delicate, pointed green leaves, lighter in colour than common spinach and with a milder taste. Cook when very fresh, preferably on the day it is bought.

WATERCHESTNUTS

Sweet, crisp white waterchestnuts have been eaten in China for centuries as a snack, having first been boiled in their skins or peeled and simmered in rock sugar. In cooked dishes they are especially popular in the south, where they are sometimes grown between rice plants in paddies. (This is why they are often muddy.) They are not part of the chestnut family at all, but an edible root or bulb about the size of a walnut that forms at the base of the stem. Tinned waterchestnuts are a pale version of the fresh ones, because both the crispness and the flavour are lost in the canning process. Fresh waterchestnuts can sometimes be obtained from Chinese grocers or good supermarkets and will keep unpeeled in a paper bag in the refrigerator for up to 2 weeks. Look for a firm, hard texture. The skin should be tight and taut, not wrinkled. If they are mushy, they are too old; feel them all over for soft, rotten spots. If you peel waterchestnuts in advance, cover with cold water to prevent browning and store in the refrigerator. If you cannot find fresh waterchestnuts, tinned ones are sold in many super-markets and Chinese grocers. Rinse well in cold water before using, and store any unused ones in the refrigerator, in a jar of water. They will keep for several weeks if you change the water daily.

SUMMER PEPPER STIR-FRY

Here is an ensemble of colours, flavours, tastes and textures that will appeal to the eye as well as the palate.

Serves 2 to 4

1 oz (25 g) Chinese dried mushrooms
2 eggs, beaten
1 teaspoon sesame oil
$\frac{1}{4}$ teaspoon salt
5 teaspoons oil, preferably groundnut
1 tablespoon finely chopped spring onions
1 tablespoon finely chopped fresh ginger
1 tablespoon finely chopped garlic
1 small fresh chilli, seeded and finely shredded
8 oz (225 g) red, yellow or green peppers (about 1 each)
2 teaspoons rice wine or dry sherry
1 teaspoon light soy sauce
1 teaspoon sugar
salt and freshly ground black pepper to taste
4 oz (110 g) bean sprouts, preferably trimmed at both ends
2 teaspoons sesame oil

Garnish
2 tablespoons finely chopped spring onions

Soak the dried mushrooms in warm water for 20 minutes or until soft. Squeeze out the excess water and cut away the stalks. Shred the mushroom caps and set aside.

Combine the beaten eggs with the 1 teaspoon sesame oil and salt in a small bowl. Heat a frying-pan or wok over moderate heat and add 2 teaspoons of the groundnut oil. Add the egg-mixture and spread over the surface of the pan until it forms a thin crêpe-like pancake. Remove from the heat and, when cool, cut the egg pancake into thin shreds and set aside.

Heat a wok or large frying-pan over high heat and add the remaining groundnut oil. Put in the spring onions, ginger, garlic and chilli and stir-fry for 30 seconds. Add the peppers, mushrooms, rice wine, soy sauce, sugar, salt and pepper. Stir-fry for 2 minutes until the peppers are soft. Stir in the bean sprouts and egg shreds and stir-fry gently for another 2 minutes, then add the 2 teaspoons sesame oil. Remove the mixture to a serving platter and garnish with the spring onions. Serve at once.

RAINBOW VEGETABLES IN LETTUCE CUPS
Photograph between pages 112 and 113

In this version of a popular Hong Kong dish, one that usually includes minced lean beef, pigeon or pork, I use only vegetables. The meat or poultry are not missed when one savours the tasty crunchiness of the vegetables combined with crispy fried bean thread noodles, cupped in a refreshing lettuce leaf and flavoured with hoisin sauce. This dish makes a good starter for a festive meal, as guests can fill their own lettuce cups at the table.

Serves 4 to 6

1 lb (450 g) iceberg lettuce
4 oz (110 g) carrots
8 oz (225 g) courgettes
4 oz (110 g) red peppers
4 oz (110 g) yellow peppers
10 fl oz (300 ml) oil, preferably groundnut, for deep-frying
1 oz (25 g) bean thread (transparent) noodles
3 tablespoons coarsely chopped garlic
$\frac{1}{2}$ teaspoon salt
2 tablespoons rice wine or dry sherry
3 tablespoons chicken or vegetable stock
4 oz (110 g) fresh or tinned waterchestnuts, coarsely chopped
2 teaspoons light soy sauce
1$\frac{1}{2}$ tablespoons oyster sauce
3 tablespoons hoisin sauce

Separate, wash and dry the lettuce leaves. Finely dice the carrots, courgettes and peppers.

 In a deep-fat fryer or large wok, heat the 10 fl oz (300 ml) of oil until almost smoking. Turn off the heat and deep-fry the noodles until they are crisp and puffed up. Drain on kitchen paper.

Heat a wok or large frying-pan and add 1 tablespoon of the oil in which you have fried the noodles. Put in the garlic, salt, carrots, rice wine and stock and stir-fry for about 2 minutes. Then add the rest of the vegetables and waterchestnuts (except the lettuce) together with the soy sauce and stir-fry for 3 minutes. Stir in the oyster sauce and continue to stir-fry for a further minute. Turn the mixture onto a platter. Arrange the lettuce and noodles on separate platters, put the hoisin sauce in a small bowl, and serve.

STIR-FRIED 'SILVER SPROUTS'

Small mung beans provide these sprouts. In Hong Kong, markets sell fresh bean sprouts plucked or trimmed at both ends. In that form they have a clean, fresh look and are ready to use, but the trimming process takes some time. They are a very nutritious addition to salads and stir-fried dishes, their mild flavour and crunchiness providing a delightful touch to every meal. When they are stir-fried with beancurd and other ingredients, as here, their colour appears as a shimmering silver, hence the name of this recipe.

Try to obtain pressed seasoned beancurd. It is cooked in a soy-flavoured sauce which also imparts a pleasant brownish colour to it. If unavailable, you may substitute fresh firm beancurd, but you must weight it down with a heavy lid for at least 2 hours to make it even firmer and less moist. It will also have less flavour, so remember to increase your seasonings. Pan-fry the beancurd until it is firm before stir-frying, otherwise it may fall apart; this will affect the appearance but not the taste.

Serves 4

1 oz (25 g) Chinese dried mushrooms
8 oz (225 g) bean sprouts
8 oz (225 g) pressed seasoned beancurd
2 oz (50 g) celery
4 oz (110 g) green peppers
2 oz (50 g) carrots
4 spring onions
1½ teaspoons salt
¼ teaspoon freshly ground black pepper
1 tablespoon oil, preferably groundnut
2 teaspoons chilli oil
2 tablespoons rice wine or dry sherry
3–4 tablespoons water

Soak the mushrooms in a large bowl of warm water for 20 minutes. Drain them and squeeze out any excess liquid. Discard the tough stalks, finely shred the caps and put them aside.

Trim the bean sprouts. Cut the pressed beancurd, celery, peppers, carrots and spring onions into fine shreds.

Heat a wok or large frying-pan over moderate heat and add the oils. Put in the salt, pepper and carrots and stir-fry for 1 minute.

Add the celery, mushrooms, beancurd, peppers and spring onions and continue to stir-fry for 2 minutes. Stir in the rice wine and water and stir-fry until most of the liquid has evaporated. Turn onto a plate and serve at once.

DRY-BRAISED BAMBOO SHOOTS WITH BROCCOLI

Fresh bamboo shoots are rare outside the Southeast Asian sub-tropics, where they feature in many recipes as a vegetable, as part of a stuffing or as a garnish for meat, seafood and vegetarian dishes. They are boiled before eating because they contain a cyanide-type poison which must be broken down. I have often wondered how it was discovered that so dangerous a food could be transformed into a delicacy – who first dared to try fresh bamboo shoots? However, those of us outside Southeast Asia must make do with the tinned variety. This is unfortunate, because fresh bamboo shoots are a true delicacy. The tinned version is an acceptable substitute but one that requires a little work to restore the flavour lost in the canning process. Served with rice, this recipe makes a light and very appetising vegetarian meal.

Serves 4

8 oz (225 g) fresh broccoli
1 lb 3 oz (540 g) tinned bamboo shoots
5 fl oz (150 ml) oil, preferably groundnut
1 teaspoon finely chopped fresh ginger
1 teaspoon salt
1 tablespoon yellow bean sauce
1 tablespoon sugar
3 tablespoons rice wine or dry sherry
5 fl oz (150 ml) chicken or vegetable stock
1 tablespoon oil, preferably groundnut
2 teaspoons finely chopped garlic

Separate the broccoli heads into florets, then peel the stalks if necessary and slice. Blanch the broccoli pieces in a large saucepan of boiling, salted water for several minutes. Drain and immerse them in cold water. Drain again thoroughly in a colander and set aside. Rinse the tinned bamboo shoots well.

Cut the bamboo shoots into $3 \times \frac{1}{2}$ inch (7.5 × 1 cm) pieces and dry thoroughly with kitchen paper. Heat the 5 fl oz (150 ml) oil in a wok or large frying-pan. Pan-fry the bamboo shoots until they are nicely brown. Drain thoroughly on kitchen paper and set aside.

Pour off all but 1 tablespoon of the oil and reheat the wok. Add the ginger, $\frac{1}{2}$ teaspoon of the salt and bean sauce, and stir-fry for 1 minute. Return the bamboo shoots to the wok and add the sugar, rice wine and stock. Braise for 3–5 minutes over high heat until most of the liquid has evaporated. Remove and set aside.

Wipe the wok clean, reheat and add the 1 tablespoon fresh oil. When smoking slightly, add the garlic, remaining salt and broccoli to the wok and stir-fry for 1 minute. Return the bamboo shoots to the wok and continue to stir-fry for another 2–3 minutes or until heated through. Turn the mixture onto a platter and serve at once.

MOCK VEGETABLE PASTA

In Chinese vegetarian cookery, a dish is not always what it appears to be. For example, 'mock duck' is taro root stuffed with minced vegetables and fried to a golden brown to look like duck. I enjoy the fun and imaginativeness of such creativity and here I take courgettes and cut them into long thin strips to look like pasta. I then salt them to remove excess moisture and, in the process, firm their texture. Quickly stir-fried with traditional Chinese seasonings, the resulting dish looks and tastes like pasta – my guests are always surprised by its lightness, flavour and texture. Do not overcook the courgettes – you want an 'al dente' firmness to the bite. This mock pasta is delicious cold, and it can also function as a vegetable or salad serving: it is perfect for picnics too.

Serves 4

2 lb (900 g) courgettes
1 tablespoon salt
1 tablespoon oil, preferably groundnut
1 tablespoon finely chopped garlic
2 teaspoons finely chopped fresh ginger
2 tablespoons finely chopped fresh coriander
2 tablespoons finely chopped spring onions, green parts only

Cut the courgettes into long thin strips resembling pasta. Put the strips into a colander and sprinkle with the salt. Leave to stand for

20 minutes. Then wrap the courgettes in a linen tea towel and squeeze out the excess liquid.

Heat a wok or large frying-pan over moderate heat and add the oil. Put in the garlic and ginger and stir-fry for 30 seconds. Add the courgettes, fresh coriander and spring onions and continue to stir-fry for 4 minutes or until the courgettes are heated through. Turn the mixture onto a platter and serve warm or at room temperature.

STIR-FRIED ASPARAGUS IN BLACK BEAN SAUCE

Asparagus is expensive even when in season, but it is so exquisite a treat it is worth buying as often as you can. Not a traditional ingredient of Southeast Asian cuisines, it has been very quickly incorporated during this century. It goes well with this pungent and robust black bean sauce, a traditional Chinese seasoning. Combined with spices, this vegetarian dish can rival any expensive meat. With rice and perhaps one other light dish, this recipe forms a complete meal for two.

Serves 2

1 lb (450 g) fresh asparagus
1 tablespoon oil, preferably groundnut
2 teaspoons finely chopped fresh ginger
2 teaspoons finely chopped garlic
2 tablespoons black beans, coarsely chopped
2 teaspoons chilli bean sauce
5 fl oz (150 ml) chicken or vegetable stock
1 teaspoon sugar
3 tablespoons rice wine or dry sherry
1 teaspoon sesame oil

Cut the asparagus diagonally into 3 inch (7.5 cm) lengths.

Heat a wok or large frying-pan and add the oil. When hot, add the ginger, garlic and black beans and stir-fry for a few seconds. Add the chilli bean sauce and, a few seconds later, add the asparagus and stir-fry for 2 minutes. Stir in the stock, sugar and rice wine. Cook the mixture over high heat for about 2 minutes, stirring continuously. Add the sesame oil, give the mixture a couple of stirs, and serve at once.

BUTTON MUSHROOMS IN OYSTER SAUCE

Button mushrooms are unknown in the East, but I have found that they, like all good edible fungi, are perfectly amenable to Chinese and other Southeast Asian spices and seasoning. Here I have combined them with the classic southern Chinese flavour of oyster sauce.

Serves 2 to 4

2 teaspoons oil, preferably groundnut
2 garlic cloves, crushed
1 lb (450 g) small whole button mushrooms
1 tablespoon dark soy sauce
1 tablespoon oyster sauce
1 teaspoon sugar
2 tablespoons rice wine or dry sherry

Heat a wok or large frying-pan and add the oil. Put in the garlic and stir-fry for 30 seconds. Add the mushrooms and stir-fry for 1 minute. Stir in the soy sauce, oyster sauce, sugar and rice wine. Turn the heat down and simmer slowly for 5 minutes, stirring from time to time. When the mushrooms are cooked, turn the heat back to high and continue stirring until most of the liquid has evaporated and the dish is ready to be served.

MU-SHU VEGETABLES WITH CHINESE PANCAKES
Photograph between pages 112 and 113

This is a vegetarian version of a traditional Chinese favourite, Mu-Shu Pork. Here, I rely upon an unusually flavourful combination of spices, vegetables and condiments which together make one forget that pork or any other meat was ever a part of the dish. Particularly important to this recipe are the Chinese dried wood ears and lily buds. These may be difficult to obtain but are worth the extra effort of searching for them. Their textures and the flavours they absorb in the stir-frying are the basis for the success of the dish. When the combined ingredients are eaten with Chinese Pancakes (page 39) and hoisin sauce, what might be an ordinary dish is transformed into a festive affair. Most of the preparation may be done ahead of time and, once the pancakes are made, the rest is easily accomplished, making this a perfect dish for a dinner party. You may experiment with your own seasonal favourite vegetables or serve with rice instead of pancakes.

Serves 4

4 eggs, beaten
4 teaspoons sesame oil
1 teaspoon salt
2 tablespoons oil, preferably groundnut
½ oz (10 g) Chinese dried wood ears
½ oz (10 g) Chinese lily buds
4 oz (110 g) red peppers
4 spring onions
3 tablespoons rice wine or dry sherry
1 tablespoon finely chopped garlic
1 tablespoon finely chopped fresh ginger
2 tablespoons dark soy sauce
6 oz (175 g) bean sprouts
Chinese Pancakes (page 39)
hoisin sauce, for dipping

Combine the beaten eggs with 2 teaspoons of the sesame oil and salt in a small bowl. Heat a frying-pan or wok over moderate heat and add 1 tablespoon of the oil. Pour in the egg mixture and spread it quickly over the surface of the pan until it forms a thin crêpe-like pancake. There is no need to turn it over. Remove from the heat and, when cool, shred the egg pancake and set aside.

Soak the dried wood ears and lily buds in warm water for about 20 minutes until soft. Meanwhile, finely shred the peppers and spring onions. Squeeze the excess liquid from the wood ears and lily buds. Finely shred the wood ears and snap off the hard ends of the lily buds.

Heat a wok or large frying-pan over high heat and add the remaining groundnut oil. When almost smoking, add the wood ears, lily buds and rice wine and stir-fry for 1 minute. Add the garlic, ginger and dark soy sauce and stir-fry for another minute. Then put in the shredded egg and bean sprouts and continue to stir-fry for 3 minutes until the ingredients are thoroughly mixed. Stir in the remaining sesame oil and turn onto a large platter. Serve with the Chinese pancakes and hoisin sauce.

VEGETABLE MEDLEY WITH TOMATO-GARLIC SAUCE

In oriental cooking, the preference is often for dipping sauces rather than for sauces that cover the food on the plate. In this recipe from Vietnam, each type of vegetable is blanched individually, thus making allowance for the different cooking requirements of each vegetable. Remember to plunge them immediately into cold water to prevent further cooking. The dipping sauce is quite lively, which is exactly what the plain, sweet, cool vegetables need. This is an ideal dish for a buffet and cocktails.

Serves 4 to 6

4 oz (110 g) Chinese long beans, runner or French beans, trimmed
4 oz (110 g) courgettes
4 oz (110 g) cauliflower
4 oz (110 g) broccoli
4 oz (110 g) carrots
4 oz (110 g) mange-tout, trimmed
1 tablespoon oil, preferably groundnut

Sauce

2 tablespoons finely chopped garlic
3 tablespoons finely chopped shallots
1 teaspoon seeded and finely chopped dried chillies
12 oz (350 g) fresh or tinned tomatoes
1 tablespoon fish sauce

Garnish

1 tablespoon finely chopped fresh coriander

Cut the beans into 3 inch (7.5 cm) lengths. Cut the courgettes into 3 inch (7.5 cm) long × $\frac{1}{2}$ inch (1 cm) wide pieces. Cut the cauliflower into small florets about 1–1$\frac{1}{2}$ inches (2.5–3.5 cm) wide. Cut off the broccoli head and break it into small florets. Peel and thinly slice the broccoli stalks. Peel and cut the carrots into 3 inch (7.5 cm) long × $\frac{1}{2}$ inch (1 cm) wide pieces.

Blanch each of the vegetables separately in a large saucepan of boiling salted water: 1 minute for the mange-tout, 2 minutes for the beans and courgettes, 4 minutes for the cauliflower, broccoli and carrots. As you take out each vegetable, plunge it into cold water until cooled, then drain well.

For the sauce, if you are using fresh tomatoes, peel, seed and cut into 1 inch (2.5 cm) cubes. If you are using tinned tomatoes, chop into small chunks. Combine the tomatoes with the rest of the sauce ingredients and purée the mixture in a blender or food processor. Arrange the vegetables on a serving platter together with the dipping sauce in a separate bowl. Garnish the sauce with the fresh coriander. Serve immediately or refrigerate and serve later.

ASPARAGUS WITH CHINESE BLACK MUSHROOMS

Asparagus is a vegetable which readily combines with many other foods in the most congenial fashion. Here, it is joined with meaty, smokey Chinese dried mushrooms, with both vegetables absorbing the essences of each other and of the sauce. I suggest that, if available, you use a larger variety of asparagus. This is a wholesome and satisfying dish, easy to prepare and, with rice, a meal in itself.

Serves 2 to 4

1 lb (450 g) large asparagus
1 oz (25 g) Chinese dried mushrooms
1 tablespoon oil, preferably groundnut
2 cloves garlic, lightly crushed
$\frac{1}{4}$ teaspoon salt
5 fl oz (150 ml) chicken or vegetable stock
2 tablespoons oyster sauce
1 teaspoon cornflour mixed with 1 teaspoon cold water

Cut the asparagus diagonally into 2 inch (5 cm) lengths, discarding the hard woody ends.

Soak the dried mushrooms in warm water for about 20 minutes. Remove the mushrooms from the water and squeeze out any excess liquid. Cut off the stalks and discard them.

Heat a wok or large frying-pan over moderate heat and add the oil. Put in the garlic, salt and asparagus and stir-fry for 1 minute. Add the stock and mushrooms and continue to stir-fry for 3 minutes or until the asparagus is cooked. Add the oyster sauce and blended cornflour and continue to cook until the sauce has been reduced to a glaze. Give the mixture a final stir, turn into a platter and serve at once.

VEGETABLE TEMPURA
Photograph between pages 112 and 113

Of all deep-fried foods, I prefer Japanese tempura. The delicate coating of batter allows the fresh vegetable flavours to come through; there is crispness without the heaviness generally associated with batter-fried foods. The secret of tempura's lace-like quality lies in the use of a thin batter made with *very* cold or iced water and not mixed together until the very last moment. Although tempura is commonly used with seafood such as prawns, it works as deliciously with vegetables. Cooking the tempura, by dipping the prepared vegetables in the batter and deep-frying them quickly, takes a bit of practice. The tempura must be served immediately. For an authentic Japanese taste, use dashi (page 16), an essential in Japanese cuisine, in preference to stock in the dipping sauce.

Serves 6–8

4 oz (110 g) cauliflower
4 oz (110 g) courgettes
4 oz (110 g) carrots
4 oz (110 g) aubergines
2 oz (50 g) Chinese long beans, runner beans or French beans, trimmed
1 small onion
4 oz (110 g) small whole button mushrooms
1 pint (570 ml) oil, preferably groundnut, for deep-frying

Sauce
2 fl oz (50 ml) dashi (page 16) or chicken or vegetable stock
3 tablespoons sake, rice wine or dry sherry
2 tablespoons light soy sauce
1 tablespoon sugar

Batter
1 egg, beaten
5 fl oz (150 ml) very cold water
4 oz (110 g) plain flour, sifted
$\frac{1}{2}$ teaspoon baking powder

Cut the cauliflower into small florets about $1–1\frac{1}{2}$ inches (3.5 cm) wide. Cut the courgettes, carrots and aubergines into thin 4 inch (10 cm) long slices. Cut the beans into 4 inch (10 cm) lengths. Thinly slice the onion.

In a small pan, simmer the sauce ingredients together for 5

minutes. Remove the sauce from the heat, leave to cool, then pour the sauce into a small serving bowl and set aside.

Combine the batter ingredients together in a bowl and quickly strain through a fine sieve. (Do this just before you are about to deep-fry, while the oil is heating.)

Heat the oil in a deep-fat fryer or large wok until hot. Dip the vegetables in the batter and fry until golden and crispy. Remove with a slotted spoon and drain on kitchen paper. You will have to do this in several batches. Serve immediately with the dipping sauce.

GREEN BEANS IN PUNGENT SAUCE

I often enjoyed this easy-to-make homely dish as a child. Fresh green beans are a nutritious and inexpensive vegetable and lend themselves to spices and seasonings that complement their delicate flavour. In this recipe, the pungent spiciness of fermented chilli beancurd turns the vegetable into something quite special. You will find fermented beancurd at Chinese grocers: you may choose from various types, ranging from mild to quite spicy. In using so lively a spice as chilli beancurd, remember that a little goes a long way.

Serves 2 to 4

1 tablespoon oil, preferably groundnut
2 garlic cloves, crushed
1 tablespoon fermented chilli beancurd
¼ teaspoon salt
1 lb (450 g) Chinese long beans or runner beans, trimmed and
  sliced, or French beans, trimmed and left whole
3 tablespoons rice wine or dry sherry
2 tablespoons water

Heat a wok or large frying-pan and add the oil. When moderately hot, add the garlic, beancurd and salt and stir-fry for about 30 seconds. Add the beans, rice wine and water and continue to stir-fry over a moderately high heat for about 5 minutes or until the beans are thoroughly cooked, adding more water if necessary to keep the beans moist. Serve at once.

SICHUAN FRIED AUBERGINES

Aubergines are delicious when fried in a light batter, which prevents too much oil penetrating the aubergines. They are then enlivened by what the Chinese call a 'fish flavouring' sauce, a non-fishy mixture of spices and seasonings normally used in the preparation of fish. Both the aubergines and the batter readily absorb the sauce. This sauce is not to be confused with the commercially bottled fish sauce (page 22) widely used in Southeast Asian cooking. Try to buy Chinese aubergines as they have a more delicate taste; however, ordinary aubergines will suffice. This is an excellent starter. If you serve it with cocktails, serve the sauce separately.

Serves 4 to 6

1 lb (450 g) aubergines
15 fl oz (400 ml) oil, preferably groundnut, for deep-frying

Batter
2 oz (50 g) plain flour
5 fl oz (150 ml) water
¼ teaspoon salt

Sauce
1 tablespoon oil, preferably groundnut
3 tablespoons finely chopped spring onions
1 tablespoon finely chopped fresh ginger
2 teaspoons chilli bean sauce
5 fl oz (150 ml) chicken or vegetable stock
2 tablespoons rice wine or dry sherry
1 tablespoon Chinese black rice vinegar or cider vinegar
3 tablespoons tomato purée
2 teaspoons sugar
2 tablespoons dark soy sauce
1 teaspoon cornflour mixed with 1 teaspoon water

Cut the aubergines into 1½ × 3 inch (3.5 × 7.5 cm) slices. Do not peel them.

For the batter, mix the flour, water and salt together in a small bowl, then strain through a fine sieve. Leave to rest for about 20 minutes.

For the sauce, heat a wok or large frying-pan until hot and add the 1 tablespoon oil. Put in the spring onions, ginger and chilli bean sauce and stir-fry for 30 seconds. Then add the stock, rice wine, vinegar, tomato purée, sugar and soy sauce and continue to cook for 1 minute. Thicken the sauce with the blended cornflour and cook for another minute. Set aside.

Heat the oil in a deep-fat fryer or large wok until quite hot. Dip the slices of aubergine into the batter, let the excess batter drip off, then deep-fry. You may have to do this in several batches. Remove from the oil with a slotted spoon and drain well on kitchen paper.

Arrange the aubergine slices on a serving platter, pour the sauce over and serve.

STIR-FRIED LETTUCE

Lettuce is used so often in the West as a garnish and salad that one tends to forget it is a vegetable and, as such, capable of a greater culinary role. As a child at home, I ate only cooked lettuce and I was a bit put off to see my Western friends eating it raw in their lunch sandwiches. In Hong Kong, the street-side food vendors or food stalls offer stir-fried lettuce as a vegetable dish to accompany rice and chicken dishes. It works very well, provided you use firm lettuce and stir-fry it very quickly.

Serves 2 to 4

1 lb (450 g) iceberg or cos lettuce
1 tablespoon oil, preferably groundnut
2 garlic cloves, crushed
1 teaspoon finely chopped fresh ginger
3 tablespoons chicken or vegetable stock
1 tablespoon light soy sauce
$\frac{1}{4}$ teaspoon salt
1 teaspoon sugar
$\frac{1}{2}$ teaspoon cornflour mixed with 1 teaspoon water

Separate the lettuce leaves and wash well. Cut the large leaves in half.

Heat a wok or large frying-pan and add the oil. When moderately hot, add the garlic and ginger and stir-fry for 30 seconds. Next add the lettuce and stir-fry quickly for a few seconds. Stir in the rest of the ingredients, except the cornflour mixture. Give a couple of stirs and then remove the lettuce to a platter with a slotted spoon. Add the blended cornflour to the sauce and bring to the boil. When the sauce thickens, pour over the lettuce and serve at once.

BITTER MELON WITH BLACK BEAN SAUCE

Bitter melon, a type of squash, is one of my favourite Chinese vegetables. True, it has a bitter quinine taste which even many Chinese do not like, but then many Westerners do not like caviar. In China, it is used in its unripe stage, when it is light green and bumpy. There are many ways to prepare it – my mother had a dozen recipes – but the most usual is to cut it up and stir-fry, as in this classic southern Chinese recipe. Look for the riper, softer, orange coloured melons, which tend to be less bitter; the blanching process also reduces the bitterness. In cooking, as often happens, the bitterness is transformed into 'bite' for, while the melon brings out the best flavours of the other ingredients, they in turn seem to neutralise some of its tartness. The result is a surprisingly refreshing effect on the palate. Bitter melon is a taste worth acquiring.

Serves 2 to 4

1 lb (450 g) bitter melon
1 tablespoon oil, preferably groundnut
1½ tablespoons black beans, coarsely chopped
1 tablespoon finely chopped fresh ginger
2 teaspoons finely chopped garlic
1 tablespoon finely chopped spring onions
2 teaspoons light soy sauce
1 tablespoon rice wine or dry sherry
1 teaspoon sugar
5 fl oz (150 ml) chicken or vegetable stock

Slice the bitter melon in half lengthways and, using a teaspoon, remove the seeds. Slice the flesh widthwise into about ¼ inch (0.5 cm) pieces. Blanch the bitter melon pieces in a large saucepan of boiling water for 2 minutes. Drain, plunge them into cold water, then drain in a colander.

Heat a wok or large frying-pan and add the oil. When moderately hot, add the black beans, ginger, garlic and spring onions and stir-fry for 30 seconds. Stir in the soy sauce, rice wine, sugar and stock. Bring the mixture to the boil and add the bitter melon. Continue to cook over high heat for about 3 minutes or until the bitter melon is completely cooked and soft. Serve at once.

CLOUD EARS STIR-FRIED WITH MANGE-TOUT

This is a colourful and wholesome vegetable dish that is easily assembled for a family dinner. It is a classic combination of the tastes and textures so typical of Chinese cookery. The cloud ears have little flavour of their own but, like mushrooms in general, they readily absorb other flavours and retain their chewy texture. And, like truffles in French cuisine, cloud ears enhance an entire recipe, bringing out the best in the other foods.

Serves 4

$\frac{1}{2}$ oz (10 g) Chinese dried cloud ears (black fungus)
4 oz (110 g) fresh or tinned (drained weight) waterchestnuts
4 oz (110 g) celery
1 tablespoon oil, preferably groundnut
2 garlic cloves, crushed
8 oz (225 g) mange-tout, trimmed

Sauce

1 tablespoon oyster sauce
1 teaspoon light soy sauce
2 teaspoons dark soy sauce
1 teaspoon sugar
2 teaspoons rice wine or dry sherry
2 teaspoons sesame oil
5 fl oz (150 ml) chicken or vegetable stock
2 teaspoons cornflour mixed with 2 teaspoons water

Soak the cloud ears in warm water for 20 minutes until soft. Set them aside.

If you are using fresh waterchestnuts, peel them. If you are using tinned waterchestnuts, drain them well and rinse in cold water. Thinly slice the waterchestnuts. String the celery and slice diagonally.

Heat a wok or large frying-pan over a medium heat and add the oil. When hot, add the garlic and stir-fry for 30 seconds. Then add the cloud ears and celery and stir-fry for 2 minutes. Stir in the mange-tout and fresh waterchestnuts and stir-fry for another minute. Add all the sauce ingredients, except the blended cornflour. Bring the sauce to the boil and stir in the cornflour mixture. If you are using tinned waterchestnuts, add at this stage and warm through. Turn the mixture onto a serving platter and serve at once.

CLOUD EARS IN HOISIN SAUCE

In this recipe, cloud ears are stir-fried in the strongly flavoured hoisin sauce, which is absorbed thoroughly while the cloud ears still retain their chewy texture. If you wish, you may add another vegetable such as cauliflower or broccoli; but by themselves the cloud ears, given zest by the rich sauce, work very well as a vegetable dish for any meal.

Serves 4

1 oz (25 g) Chinese dried cloud ears (black fungus)
1 tablespoon oil, preferably groundnut
2 garlic cloves, crushed
$\frac{1}{4}$ teaspoon salt
3 tablespoons rice wine or dry sherry
10 fl oz (300 ml) chicken or vegetable stock
1 tablespoon light soy sauce
3 tablespoons hoisin sauce
2 teaspoons sesame oil
1 teaspoon cornflour mixed with 1 teaspoon water

Soak the dried cloud ears in warm water for 20 minutes until soft. Rinse in cold water and drain in a colander.

Heat a wok or frying-pan until hot and add the oil and garlic. Stir-fry for 30 seconds, then add the cloud ears. Continue to stir-fry for another 2 minutes. Stir in the rest of the ingredients, except for the cornflour mixture. Continue to cook for another 2 minutes, add the blended cornflour and, when the sauce thickens, the dish is ready to be served.

GRILLED MUSHROOMS WITH LEMON SAUCE

This recipe is of Japanese origin, simple but unusual and quite delicious. It offers a different way to enjoy fresh mushrooms and is a perfect side dish to enliven a barbecue or as an accompaniment to grilled meats or poultry. The mushrooms may also be cooked under the grill, so the dish may be savoured indoors during the winter as well, missing only the smokey barbecue flavour. For an authentic taste, try to obtain Japanese sake for the sauce; if it cannot be found, rice wine or dry sherry are acceptable substitutes. The lemon sauce can be made beforehand.

Serves 4

1 lb (450 g) large button mushrooms
2 teaspoons salt

Sauce
2 tablespoons lemon juice
1 tablespoon dark soy sauce
1 tablespoon sake, rice wine or dry sherry
2 teaspoons sugar
2 tablespoons finely chopped spring onions

Sprinkle the mushrooms with the salt and mix well. Put the mushrooms into a colander and leave to drain for 20 minutes. When the mushrooms have drained, rinse them in water and blot dry with kitchen paper.

Heat the sauce ingredients together in a small saucepan until the sugar dissolves. Leave to cool.

Soak some wooden skewers in cold water for 5 minutes. Thread 3 or 4 mushrooms on each skewer and cook under the grill or on a barbecue. When they are cooked, remove from the skewers, mix with the sauce and serve.

STIR-FRIED CUCUMBERS

Cucumbers are too often taken for granted, their cool unobtrusive virtues having rendered them less interesting than other vegetables and fit only for salad. Stir-fried, however, they take on an unexpected boldness. My uncle used to cook them with little pieces of pork, but I have learned that they are tasty all by themselves with a complementary sauce. Salt the cucumbers first to rid them of their excess liquid. Stir-fried and made savoury by the sauce, the cucumbers make a wonderful vegetable side dish that is ideal for lunch or dinner.

Serves 4

1½ lb (700 g) cucumbers (about 2 small)
2¼ teaspoons salt
1 tablespoon oil, preferably groundnut
2 tablespoons dark soy sauce
1 tablespoon rice wine or dry sherry
2 teaspoons sesame oil
1 teaspoon chilli oil

Peel the cucumbers, slice them in half lengthways and, using a teaspoon, remove the seeds. Cut the cucumber halves into 3 inch (7.5 cm) lengths. Sprinkle them with 2 teaspoons of the salt and mix well. Put the salted cucumbers into a colander and leave for 20 minutes to drain. This rids the cucumbers of any excess liquid. When the cucumber pieces have drained, rinse in water and then blot dry with kitchen paper.

Heat a wok or large frying-pan until hot and add the oil. Put in the cucumber and stir-fry for 2 minutes. Stir in the remaining salt, soy sauce and rice wine and continue to stir-fry for another 2 minutes. Add the sesame and chilli oils and give the mixture several good stirs. Serve at once.

STIR-FRIED SPICY CARROTS

The European carrot is now the standard in China and in Chinese cookery, although the Chinese do cultivate a larger version which is also quite sweet. Because of their distinctive taste and colour, carrots combine well with other seasonings and herbs, in this case the pungent flavours of ginger, black beans, garlic and dried chillies. The carrots are first roll cut (see page 32) and then blanched. The final step of stir-frying sears the spices and allows the carrots to absorb the new flavours. These colourful and tasty carrots go well with a simple serving of plain rice or as a pleasing vegetable dish accompanying meat or poultry. They can also be served at room temperature, making them an interesting addition to any picnic menu.

Serves 4

1½ lb (700 g) carrots
1 tablespoon oil, preferably groundnut
2 teaspoons finely chopped garlic
1 teaspoon finely chopped fresh ginger
2 dried chillies, seeded
1 tablespoon black beans, coarsely chopped
1 teaspoon sugar
2 tablespoons rice wine or dry sherry
2 teaspoons sesame oil

Peel the carrots and roll cut according to the technique on page 32. Blanch the carrots in a large saucepan of boiling salted water for 4–5 minutes, then immerse them in cold water. Drain thoroughly.

Heat a wok or large frying-pan until moderately hot and add the oil. Put in the garlic, ginger, chillies and black beans and stir-fry for about 1 minute. Stir in the carrots, sugar and rice wine and continue to stir-fry for about 3 minutes or until the carrots are thoroughly heated. Add the sesame oil and continue to stir-fry for 20 seconds.

CRISPY SPRING ONION OMELETTE

Here the mildness and soft texture of the eggs are transformed by the cooking process and the addition of other textures and seasonings. My mother often prepared just such a dish when she was in a hurry, as it was quick and economical. It would be served over rice, with a touch of oyster sauce.

Serves 2

6 spring onions
$\frac{1}{2}$ oz (10 g) fresh chilli
6 eggs, beaten
1 tablespoon sesame oil
3 tablespoons finely chopped spring onions
$\frac{1}{2}$ teaspoon salt
2 teaspoons light soy sauce
4 tablespoons oil, preferably groundnut

Garnish
1 tablespoon finely chopped fresh coriander

Cut the spring onions diagonally into 2 inch (5 cm) lengths. Finely shred the chilli. In a large bowl, mix the eggs, sesame oil, finely chopped spring onions, salt and soy sauce.

Heat a wok or large frying-pan over high heat and add 1 tablespoon of the oil. Put in the spring onion pieces and chilli and stir-fry for 2 minutes. Remove them and wipe the wok clean. Reheat the wok and add the 3 tablespoons oil and, when hot, add the egg mixture. When the egg begins to cook, return the cooked spring onions and chilli to the wok and continue to cook over high heat for 2 minutes until brown and crispy. Flip the omelette over and brown the other side. Remove to a platter and garnish with the coriander. Serve at once.

BRAISED CHINESE MUSHROOMS
Photograph between pages 112 and 113 and opposite page 144

Chinese family banquets, held on special occasions, are truly feasts. As a boy attending such gala affairs, I always looked for the large plate of beautifully arranged, thick Chinese mushrooms that traditionally graced the table. Braised in a rich sauce, smokey in taste, chewy in texture, these mushrooms were a great favourite of mine. I ate them whenever I could, as any Western youth might eat crisps or roasted peanuts. The large dried variety of Chinese mushrooms recommended for this recipe can be expensive, but they are well worth it for a special occasion. Do not cut up the caps, as left whole they absorb the sauce better. The dish reheats beautifully, which makes it ideal for a large dinner party as it can be prepared in advance.

Serves 4

4 oz (110 g) large Chinese dried mushrooms
1 tablespoon oil, preferably groundnut

Sauce
10 fl oz (300 ml) chicken or vegetable stock
2 tablespoons dark soy sauce
2 tablespoons sugar
2 teaspoons sesame oil
1 tablespoon rice wine or dry sherry

Garnish
2 spring onions, sliced

Soak the dried mushrooms in warm water for 20 minutes until soft. Squeeze the excess liquid from the mushrooms and remove and discard the stalks. Leave the mushrooms whole.

Heat a wok or large frying-pan and add the oil. Put in the mushrooms and stir-fry for a few seconds. Quickly add the sauce ingredients and turn the heat down. Braise the mushrooms for 7 minutes, stirring continually, until the mushrooms have absorbed most of the sauce. Turn the mixture onto a serving platter and garnish with the spring onions.

EGGS WITH CHINESE MUSHROOMS

Eggs are popular in Eastern vegetarian cookery. In China, the tradition is always to contrast the softness of the eggs with firm, crunchy or crisp textures. In this recipe, I combine two varieties of dried firm mushrooms, one of them cloud ears, with eggs. Do try to obtain the Chinese dried variety. You may substitute fresh button mushrooms, but be sure to cook them until most of the moisture has gone. This is an easy-to-prepare dish and goes wonderfully with rice or as a filling for Chinese Pancakes (page 39).

Serves 4

1 oz (25 g) Chinese dried mushrooms
$\frac{1}{2}$ oz (10 g) Chinese dried cloud ears (black fungus)
8 oz (225 g) yellow onions
4 eggs, beaten
$2\frac{1}{2}$ teaspoons salt
1 tablespoon sesame oil
3 tablespoons oil, preferably groundnut
2 tablespoons rice wine or dry sherry
1 tablespoon light soy sauce
3 tablespoons chicken or vegetable stock

Garnish
3 tablespoons chopped spring onions
1 teaspoon sesame oil

Soak the Chinese dried mushrooms and cloud ears in separate bowls of warm water for about 20 minutes, then drain. Rinse the cloud ears well and leave whole. Squeeze out any excess liquid from the dried mushrooms, discard the tough stalks, then shred the caps and set aside. Finely slice the onions. Combine the eggs with 2 teaspoons of the salt and sesame oil in a small bowl.

Heat a wok or large frying-pan over high heat and add 1 tablespoon of the oil. Put in the onions and stir-fry for 4 minutes until soft and translucent. Remove them and wipe the wok clean. Reheat the wok over high heat and add the remaining oil. Add the mushrooms, cloud ears, rice wine, soy sauce and remaining salt and stir-fry for 2 minutes. Stir in the stock and return the cooked onions to the wok. Continue to stir-fry for 1 minute. Then add the egg mixture and stir several times. The dish is ready when the eggs have set. Transfer to a platter and garnish with the spring onions and sesame oil.

CRISPY VEGETABLE STIR-FRY

I like to serve meals that appeal to the eye as well as to the palate. Therefore, when peppers are in season I use them as often as possible: the sweetness of the reds and yellows and the mild bite of the greens delight one's senses and add a colourful dimension to any meal. Stir-frying preserves the best characteristics of peppers. When combined, as here, with the crisp texture and sweet flavour of bamboo shoots and waterchestnuts and the zing of ginger, the result is a colourful and healthy vegetable dish. Use fresh waterchestnuts if possible.

Remember that the key to stir-frying vegetables is to cook the harder ones, or those with the least amount of moisture, first.

Serves 4

4 oz (110 g) red peppers
4 oz (110 g) green peppers
4 oz (110 g) yellow peppers
4 oz (110 g) fresh or tinned (drained weight) waterchestnuts
2 oz (50 g) tinned (drained weight) bamboo shoots
2 teaspoons oil, preferably groundnut
2 teaspoons salt
3 slices fresh ginger
2 oz (50 g) mange-tout, trimmed
3 tablespoons water

Cut the peppers into 1½ inch (3.5 cm) triangles. Thinly slice the waterchestnuts and bamboo shoots.

Heat a wok or large frying-pan and add the oil. When moderately hot, add the salt and ginger and stir-fry for about 1 minute to allow the ginger to flavour the oil. Add the peppers and stir-fry for 2 minutes. Stir in the waterchestnuts and bamboo shoots and continue to stir-fry for 2 minutes. Finally add the mange-tout and stir-fry for 30 seconds, then add the water. Stir-fry for another minute or until the mange-tout are cooked, adding more water if necessary. When the vegetables are cooked, serve them at once.

Opposite: *Spicy Citrus-Flavoured Noodles (page 155) and Southeast Asian Noodle Salad (page 152)*
Overleaf: *Vegetable Tempura (page 100); Rainbow Vegetables in Lettuce Cups (page 91), Braised Chinese Mushrooms (page 110) and Mu-Shu Vegetables (page 96) with Chinese Pancakes (page 39)*

VIETNAMESE-STYLE VEGETABLES

This is a home-style family dish that is also served in Vietnamese restaurants. Its main ingredients are nutritious beancurd and mushrooms, combined with cauliflower, which provides a new texture and flavour, and a spicy fish sauce to enliven the dish. The beancurd, cut into thin strips and deep-fried, does not break up when stir-fried. Serve this substantial dish with plain rice and you have a complete meal.

Serves 4

8 oz (225 g) fresh beancurd
10 fl oz (300 ml) oil, preferably groundnut, for deep-frying
4 oz (110 g) cauliflower
1½ tablespoons oil, preferably groundnut
2 garlic cloves, crushed
2 tablespoons finely chopped shallots
8 oz (225 g) small button mushrooms
½ teaspoon salt
5 fl oz (150 ml) water
1 tablespoon light soy sauce
2 teaspoons fish sauce
3 tablespoons finely chopped fresh coriander

Cut the beancurd into 3 × ½ inch (7.5 × 1 cm) strips.

Heat the 10 fl oz (300 ml) oil in a deep-fat fryer or a large wok until it almost smokes. Deep-fry the beancurd strips in 2 batches. When each batch is light brown, remove and drain the beancurd well on kitchen paper.

Cut the cauliflower into small florets about 1–1½ inches (2.5–3.5 cm) wide. Blanch the florets in a large saucepan of boiling salted water for several minutes, then immerse in cold water and drain thoroughly.

Heat a wok or large frying-pan and add the 1½ tablespoons oil. Put in the garlic and shallots and stir-fry for 30 seconds. Then add the mushrooms, salt, water, soy sauce and fish sauce and stir-fry for 5 minutes. Gently stir in the beancurd, cauliflower and fresh coriander and continue to stir-fry for 2 minutes or until the cauli-flower and beancurd are heated through. It is then ready to serve.

Opposite: *Fragrant Coconut Rice (page 167) and Pineapple Fried Rice (page 166)*

FIVE

BEANCURD DISHES

Of all vegetarian foods, beancurd (page 12) is the most versatile and important in oriental cookery. High in protein but low in cholesterol, plain but absorbent, soft-textured but strong, it is nutritious and receptive to all types of cooking. Beancurd can be boiled, simmered, steamed, braised, deep-fried, pan-fried or used as a filling. Adding substance without an intrusive taste, it combines well with all foods. Moreover, it is quite inexpensive. In fact, beancurd represents such a good buy that the slang expression in eastern Chinese dialects for easily taking advantage of a person is 'eating beancurd'. It is known as doufu in Chinese or tofu in Japanese.

The many techniques and combinations for cooking beancurd are represented in this chapter. It can be simply simmered as in Beancurd Custard in Oyster Sauce, or deep-fried as in Crispy Beancurd Cubes with Peanut Dipping Sauce, or braised in a Southeast Asian-style sauce as in Coconut-Stewed Beancurd and Vegetables. Tasting beancurd in so many different forms will persuade even the most sceptical of its wonderful properties.

GRILLED BEANCURD SHISH KEBABS
Photograph opposite page 81

In this recipe, the beancurd readily absorbs the marinade and then grills perfectly. This is really an East–West combination, inspired by a wonderful vegetarian restaurant in San Francisco called Greens. Always buy the freshest beancurd. For this recipe you will need the firm variety, as soft beancurd is not suitable for skewering. You can add other vegetables such as small tomatoes, peppers and onions to make real shish kebabs. This is an excellent side dish or makes a perfect starter with drinks.

Serves 2 to 4

1 lb (450 g) firm beancurd

Marinade
3 tablespoons light soy sauce
1 tablespoon sesame paste or peanut butter
1 tablespoon chilli bean sauce
1 tablespoon Chinese white rice vinegar or cider vinegar
1 tablespoon rice wine or dry sherry

Place the beancurd between several layers of kitchen paper with a heavy weight on top, such as a heavy lid. Leave the beancurd to stand for 1 hour.

Mix all the marinade ingredients together in a small bowl. Cut the beancurd into 2 inch (5 cm) cubes and add to the marinade. Marinate the cubes for 1 hour, or longer for a stronger flavour, turning them at least once.

Meanwhile, soak some wooden skewers in cold water for 5 minutes. Thread the beancurd cubes on the skewers, taking care to put no more than 3 to 4 on each skewer. Cook the beancurd cubes under the grill or on a barbecue, 2–3 minutes on each side or until brown, basting once with the marinade. Serve with your choice of dipping sauces (page 22).

HOME-STYLE SPICY BEANCURD

This recipe is my adaptation of 'Ma Po's home-cooked beancurd', a popular and traditional Sichuan dish I first experienced in a Sichuan-style restaurant in Hong Kong. The Sichuan style empha-sises hot spices and strong seasonings, with which beancurd readily combines. I have made this into a vegetarian dish by omit-ting the minced beef or pork that is normally used. Beancurd is such a good protein and the sauce and garnish are so full of flavour that the meat is not missed, either nutritionally or as a taste. Note that here I use *soft* beancurd, so that the result is a spicy and savoury custard-like dish, perfect with rice, crispy noodles or bread.

Serves 2 to 4

1 lb (450 g) soft beancurd, drained
1 tablespoon oil, preferably groundnut
1 tablespoon finely chopped fresh ginger
1 tablespoon finely chopped garlic
1 tablespoon chilli bean sauce
1 teaspoon yellow bean sauce
2 teaspoons sugar
2 fl oz (50 ml) chicken or vegetable stock
2 tablespoons rice wine or dry sherry
1 teaspoon cornflour mixed with 1 teaspoon water

Garnish

2 teaspoons sesame oil
2 tablespoons finely chopped spring onions

Cut the beancurd into 1 inch (2.5 cm) cubes and set aside. Heat a wok or large frying-pan over high heat and add the oil. Put in the ginger, garlic, chilli bean sauce and yellow bean sauce and stir-fry for 30 seconds. Add the sugar, stock and rice wine and cook for 2 minutes. Stir the blended cornflour into the wok. When the sauce has slightly thickened, add the beancurd cubes and stir gently. Continue to cook for 2 minutes or until the beancurd is heated through. Garnish and serve at once.

SWEET AND SOUR BEANCURD

Sweet and sour sauces must never be too sweet or too vinegary. When properly made they are a delight. As the contrasting tastes alternate and combine on the palate, one understands why well-prepared sweet and sour dishes are justly praised classics. Such a sauce lends itself to many different types of food but combines particularly well with beancurd. Here the beancurd is deep-fried, giving it an interesting spongy texture and enhancing its absorbent nature. The sweet pineapple both balances and emphasises the rich, tangy, sour sharpness of the sauce. This unusual, nutritious dish reheats well and may be made well in advance. Serve it with rice for a complete meal.

Serves 2 to 4

1 lb (450 g) firm beancurd
10 fl oz (300 ml) oil, preferably groundnut, for deep-frying
2 oz (50 g) carrots
2 oz (50 g) red pepper
1 lb (450 g) fresh pineapple or 10 oz (275 g) tinned pineapple

Sauce
2 garlic cloves, crushed
2 tablespoons tomato purée
1 tablespoon finely chopped lemongrass (optional)
1 tablespoon white rice vinegar or cider vinegar
2 tablespoons rice wine or dry sherry
1 tablespoon light soy sauce
1 tablespoon sugar
5 fl oz (150 ml) chicken or vegetable stock
2 teaspoons cornflour mixed with 2 teaspoons water

Garnish
fresh coriander leaves

Cut the beancurd into 1 inch (2.5 cm) cubes. Heat the oil in a deep-fat fryer or large wok. When the oil is almost smoking, deep-fry the beancurd cubes. You may have to do this in several batches. Drain on kitchen paper and set aside.

Cut the carrots into 1 inch (2.5 cm) rounds and blanch in a small saucepan of boiling water for 3 minutes. Drain and set aside. Cut the pepper into 1 inch (2.5 cm) squares. Peel, core and cut the pineapple into 1 inch (2.5 cm) cubes.

Combine the sauce ingredients together in a large saucepan and bring to the boil. Add the carrot and red pepper and stir well. Stir the blended cornflour into the sauce and bring it back to the boil. Reduce the heat to simmering point and gently put in the beancurd and pineapple. Mix well, then turn the mixture onto a deep platter. Garnish and serve at once.

SIMPLE BEANCURD AND MUSHROOM STIR-FRY

In this healthy family dish, the lightly fried beancurd with a slightly crispy surface sets off the texture of the braised mushrooms perfectly. Remember to fry the delicate beancurd squares gently. This dish reheats well and is even better the second day, although of course some of the crispness will be lost.

Serves 2 to 4

1 lb (450 g) firm beancurd
4 tablespoons oil, preferably groundnut
2 cloves garlic, crushed
¼ teaspoon salt
8 oz (225 g) small whole button mushrooms

Sauce

1 tablespoon dark soy sauce
2 tablespoons rice wine or dry sherry
2 tablespoons sugar
2 tablespoons chicken or vegetable stock

Garnish

2 spring onions, diagonally sliced

Cut the beancurd into 2 inch (5 cm) squares, ½ inch (1 cm) thick.
Heat a wok or large frying-pan and add 3 tablespoons of the oil. When the oil is hot, fry the beancurd on each side until golden

brown. You may have to do this in several batches. Drain on kitchen paper.

Drain the oil and wipe the wok clean. Reheat the wok over moderate heat and add the remaining tablespoon of oil. Put in the garlic and salt and stir-fry for 30 seconds. Stir in the mushrooms and the sauce ingredients. Cook over moderate heat for 5 minutes or until the mushrooms are cooked. Return the beancurd to the wok and, once heated through, garnish and serve.

STUFFED BEANCURD SQUARES

Beancurd suffers from an undeserved reputation for excessive blandness and dullness. It is indeed bland (and so is rice), but this is a virtue when properly approached. The trick is to take advantage of beancurd's generous receptivity to other foods, spices and seasonings. In this recipe, which my cooking colleague Gordon Wing helped to create, we stuffed the beancurd with a mixture of ginger, mushrooms, onions and other flavours and textures, then pan-fried and covered the beancurd squares with a savoury sauce. Serve with rice.

Serves 2 to 4

1 lb (450 g) firm beancurd
3–4 tablespoons oil, preferably groundnut

Filling
$\frac{1}{2}$ oz (10 g) Chinese dried mushrooms
1 teaspoon finely chopped spring onions
$\frac{1}{2}$ teaspoon finely chopped fresh ginger
3 tablespoons roasted peanuts, coarsely chopped
$\frac{1}{2}$ teaspoon salt
$\frac{1}{2}$ teaspoon pepper
1 teaspoon sugar
1 teaspoon yellow bean sauce
2 tablespoons coarsely chopped garlic
$\frac{1}{2}$ teaspoon Sichuan peppercorns, roasted and ground (page 24)

Sauce
1 tablespoon oyster sauce
1 tablespoon light soy sauce
1 tablespoon rice wine or dry sherry
$\frac{1}{2}$ teaspoon cornflour mixed with 3 tablespoons water

Soak the dried mushrooms in a bowl of warm water for 20 minutes. Drain and squeeze out any excess liquid. Cut off and discard the stalks; coarsely chop the mushroom caps.

Cut the beancurd into 4 pieces to make squares. With a teaspoon, scoop out 1 tablespoon beancurd from the top, without breaking through to the bottom. You will now have a square of beancurd with a dip in the centre of the top. This is where the filling will go.

Heat a wok or large frying-pan over moderate heat and add 1 tablespoon of the oil. Put in the filling ingredients and stir-fry for 2 minutes. Leave the mixture to cool, then finely chop in a blender. Gently spoon the filling into the hollowed-out beancurd squares.

Heat a frying-pan or wok over high heat and add 2 tablespoons of the oil. When hot, add the stuffed beancurd squares, unfilled side down. Lower the heat and fry, turning them over from time to time until they are brown all over. You may have to do this in 2 batches, adding more oil if necessary. Remove the stuffed beancurd, drain on kitchen paper, and arrange on a serving platter.

Meanwhile, wipe out the wok and bring the sauce ingredients to simmering point, stirring. Pour this mixture over the beancurd and serve at once.

SAVOURY BEANCURD CASSEROLE

There are many different variations of beancurd, and one of the tastiest is fermented red beancurd. This impressive condiment is preserved by fermentation in a solution of red rice, salt and spices. It has a pungent aroma which dissipates as it cooks, leaving a flavour and fragrance that richly complements a stew or casserole, especially one made with beancurd. The other spices combine perfectly with the fermented beancurd and create a sauce that permeates the bean thread noodles as well. My mother often made a version of this casserole during the cold Chicago winters of my childhood. Its rich aromas and combination of flavours evoke memories of those days. This is a hearty dish that reheats easily and is perfect served over rice.

Serves 4

1 oz (25 g) Chinese dried mushrooms
12 oz (350 g) Chinese leaves or white cabbage
1 lb (450 g) firm beancurd
15 fl oz (400 ml) oil, preferably groundnut, for deep-frying
1 tablespoon oil, preferably groundnut
2 tablespoons fermented red beancurd
1 tablespoon finely chopped fresh ginger
1½ tablespoons finely chopped garlic
2 oz (50 g) bean thread (transparent) noodles
1 teaspoon salt
2 teaspoons sugar
3 tablespoons rice wine or dry sherry
1 tablespoon light soy sauce
3 tablespoons chopped spring onions
10 fl oz (300 ml) chicken or vegetable stock

Soak the dried mushrooms in warm water for about 20 minutes until soft. Squeeze the excess liquid from the mushrooms, and remove and discard the stalks. Shred the Chinese leaves or white cabbage.

Cut the beancurd into 1 inch (2.5 cm) cubes. Heat the oil in a deep-fat fryer or large wok. When the oil is almost smoking, deep-fry the beancurd cubes. You may have to do this in several batches. Remove and drain on kitchen paper.

Heat a wok or large frying-pan and add the 1 tablespoon oil. Put in the fermented beancurd, ginger and garlic and stir-fry for about 30 seconds. Add the rest of the ingredients. Bring the mixture to simmering point and add the deep-fried beancurd. Cover tightly and braise gently for about 20 minutes.

To reheat, bring to simmering point over low heat until the mixture is hot.

CANTONESE-STYLE BEANCURD WITH CHINESE GREENS

This tasty dish is a staple item on the food stalls and in the kitchens of Hong Kong. It is nutritious, inexpensive and substantial. Chinese greens have a light, earthy, fresh taste and go well with beancurd. Caramel-coloured oyster sauce is a savoury blend of oysters and selected spices with a meaty aroma. This is an easy-to-make treat, and when served with plain rice makes a full meal. You may substitute Swiss chard or spinach for the Chinese greens.

Serves 2 to 4

1 lb (450 g) firm beancurd
1 lb (450 g) Chinese greens
10 fl oz (300 ml) oil, preferably groundnut, for deep-frying
1 tablespoon oil, preferably groundnut
4 garlic cloves, crushed
3 tablespoons oyster sauce
5 fl oz (150 ml) chicken or vegetable stock
1 tablespoon cornflour mixed with 1 tablespoon water

Cut the beancurd into 1 inch (2.5 cm) cubes. Cut the Chinese greens into 3 inch (7.5 cm) pieces.

Heat the 10 fl oz (300 ml) oil in a deep-fat fryer or large wok until it almost smokes. Deep-fry the beancurd cubes in several batches. When each batch of beancurd cubes is lightly browned, about 1–2 minutes, remove and drain well on kitchen paper.

Heat a wok or large frying-pan and add the 1 tablespoon of oil. When hot, put in the garlic and Chinese greens and stir-fry for 2 minutes over high heat. Stir in the oyster sauce, stock and blended cornflour. Reduce the heat to very low and add the beancurd cubes. Simmer for 3 minutes or until the beancurd is heated through.

COCONUT-STEWED BEANCURD AND VEGETABLES

Vegetable stews enjoy an honourable place in the Chinese cuisine and are popular throughout Southeast Asia. Meat and poultry are often expensive, but the cheaper beancurd and vegetables provide a healthy and flavoursome – and in many ways even superior – substitute. They are the principal dishes today for most rural Indonesian families and, in Thailand, they are prominent among the non-curry meals available at food stalls. This unusual recipe is of Vietnamese origin. The beancurd is deep-fried and then braised with vegetables in a rich coconut milk broth flavoured with fish sauce. You may substitute other vegetables, such as Brussels sprouts, turnips or parsnips if you like – always use those that are in season. As with stews in general, vegetable stews can be made well in advance, and they taste better the day after preparation – but reheat them slowly. Serve with plain rice.

Serves 4

1 lb (450 g) firm beancurd
8 oz (225 g) cauliflower
4 oz (110 g) Chinese long beans, runner beans or French beans, trimmed
4 oz (110 g) carrots
4 oz (110 g) fresh or frozen peas
10 fl oz (300 ml) oil, preferably groundnut, for deep-frying
15 fl oz (400 ml) fresh or tinned coconut milk (page 14)
5 fl oz (150 ml) water
½ teaspoon salt
2 tablespoons dark soy sauce
2 teaspoons sugar
1 tablespoon fish sauce

Cut the beancurd into 1 inch (2.5 cm) cubes. Cut the cauliflower into small florets about 1–1½ inches (2.5–3.5 cm) wide. Slice the beans into 3 inch (7.5 cm) lengths. Peel and cut the carrots into ½ inch (1 cm) cubes. If you are using fresh peas, blanch them for 3 minutes in a saucepan of boiling water, then drain in a colander. (There is no need to blanch the frozen peas.)

Heat the oil in a deep-fat fryer or a large wok until it almost smokes. Deep-fry the beancurd cubes for 1–2 minutes in 2 batches. When each batch of beancurd cubes is lightly brown, remove and drain well on kitchen paper.

Bring the coconut milk, water, salt, soy sauce, sugar and fish sauce to the boil in a large saucepan. Reduce the heat to simmering, add the vegetables and beancurd, cover tightly and braise for about 20 minutes or until the vegetables are cooked.

RED-COOKED BEANCURD
Photograph opposite page 81

'Red-cooked' is a term applied to Chinese dishes braised and spiced with the robust, dark, brownish-red seasonings of hoisin sauce, made from soybean flour, red beans, chillies, sugar, salt, garlic and spices. The fried beancurd has a crispy surface while its soft interior readily absorbs the sauce. This is a flavourful dish that is a complete meal with other vegetable or meat dishes and plain rice.

Serves 2 to 4

1 lb (450 g) firm beancurd
3 tablespoons oil, preferably groundnut

Sauce
2 tablespoons dark soy sauce
1 tablespoon rice wine or dry sherry
2 tablespoons hoisin sauce
$\frac{1}{2}$ teaspoon Sichuan peppercorns, roasted and finely ground (page 24)
1 teaspoon chilli bean sauce
1 teaspoon sugar
2 teaspoons finely chopped fresh ginger
$\frac{1}{4}$ teaspoon salt
5 fl oz (150 ml) chicken or vegetable stock
1 tablespoon oil, preferably groundnut

Cut the beancurd into 1 inch (2.5 cm) cubes. Heat a wok or large frying-pan and add the oil. When moderately hot, add the beancurd and fry for 1–2 minutes on each side until golden brown. Set aside. Wipe the wok clean.

Add all the sauce ingredients to the wok and bring to simmering point. Return the beancurd to the wok and simmer gently in this mixture for about 5 minutes. Turn out onto a serving platter and serve at once.

CRISPY BEANCURD CUBES WITH PEANUT DIPPING SAUCE

In this delectable recipe, based on a dish I once enjoyed in Thailand, the peanut dipping sauce provides the zest and colour for the beancurd. In Thailand, roasted peanuts are pounded into a paste which is much easier to use than our peanut butter; some little bits of peanut are left in the paste to provide a crunchy texture. Here, the fried cubes of beancurd, crusty on the outside and spongy soft inside, are dipped into the peanut sauce, making a delightful starter or cocktail food. Serve the beancurd hot, as its skin toughens as it cools.

Serves 4 to 6

12 oz (350 g) firm beancurd
10 fl oz (300 ml) oil, preferably groundnut, for deep-frying

Sauce
1 oz (25 g) roasted peanuts
1 tablespoon sugar
2 tablespoons water
2 teaspoons Chinese white rice vinegar or cider vinegar
1 tablespoon finely chopped fresh coriander
½ teaspoon salt
½ teaspoon chilli oil

Cut the beancurd into 1 inch (2.5 cm) cubes. Combine the sauce ingredients together in a small bowl and set aside.

Heat the oil in a deep-fat fryer or large wok until it almost smokes. Deep-fry the beancurd cubes for 1–2 minutes in 2 batches. When each batch of beancurd cubes is lightly browned, remove and drain well on kitchen paper.

Arrange the beancurd cubes on a platter and serve the peanut sauce separately for dipping.

PAN-FRIED BEANCURD WITH LEEKS

Leeks are popular throughout China but especially in the north, where this recipe comes from. They are an ideal accompaniment to beancurd because of their texture and robust flavour. This is good, simple fare of the kind Chinese families enjoy at home. Serve with plain boiled rice.

Serves 2 to 4

1 lb (450 g) firm beancurd
3 tablespoons oil, preferably groundnut
12 oz (350 g) leeks
3 cloves garlic, crushed
1 dried chilli, seeded
2 teaspoons chilli bean sauce
1 $\frac{1}{2}$ tablespoons dark soy sauce
2 teaspoons sugar
1 tablespoon rice wine or dry sherry
5 fl oz (150 ml) chicken or vegetable stock

Cut the beancurd in half, then cut again on the diagonal into triangles. Heat a wok or large frying-pan over moderate heat and add the oil. Fry the beancurd triangles until golden brown. You may have to do this in several batches. Drain on kitchen paper.

Cut the leeks into shreds, discarding the green parts. Wash well; you may have to do this several times.

Reheat the wok over high heat. Put in the garlic and chilli and stir-fry for 30 seconds. Add the leeks and continue to stir-fry for 3 minutes, then add the rest of the ingredients. Bring the mixture to the boil. Turn the heat down to a simmer and return the beancurd triangles to the mixture. Cook for another 3 minutes or until the beancurd is heated through. Serve at once.

BEANCURD CUSTARD IN OYSTER SAUCE

For a high-protein vegetarian main dish, try this simple recipe. Served with fresh vegetables and plain rice, you have a wholesome family meal. The soft beancurd must be handled more gently than the firm variety, but it will be like eating a wonderful silky savoury custard. Always use the freshest beancurd available.

Serves 2 to 4

1 lb (450 g) soft beancurd
1 tablespoon oil, preferably groundnut
2 slices fresh ginger
2½ tablespoons oyster sauce
1 teaspoon light soy sauce
1 tablespoon rice wine or dry sherry
5 fl oz (150 ml) chicken or vegetable stock
1 teaspoon sugar
1 teaspoon cornflour mixed with 1 teaspoon water

Cut the beancurd into 1½ inch (3.5 cm) cubes.

Heat a wok or large frying-pan and add the oil. When moderately hot, add the ginger slices, oyster sauce, soy sauce, rice wine, stock and sugar and stir for 1 minute, then add the blended cornflour. When the mixture begins to thicken, add the beancurd and simmer gently to heat through. Serve at once.

SIX

HOT PASTA & NOODLES

Pasta or noodles come in many forms in China, Japan and Southeast Asia. I need only name the various types of Japanese pasta to illustrate: harusame, hiyamugi, kishimen, malfun, ramen, shira-take, soba, somen, udon. These are made from wheat, rice, buck-wheat, bean threads or yam threads. Throughout these areas, pasta is eaten in the form of noodles, wuntuns and pasta wrappers. These foods have been a part of the diet of this region for many hundreds of years.

All pasta is characterised by subtle variations of texture and colour, absorbent receptivity to sauces and congeniality to other foods, plus excellent nutritional values. Its universal popularity is therefore not surprising.

The word 'pasta' is, of course, an Italian word. I use it because it has entered our language as a generic term meaning unleavened dough, rolled out and formed into different shapes. One regional difference is that some oriental pastas are made from rice flour rather than wheat.

In this book, I have combined various pastas with spices and flavours typical of China, Japan and Southeast Asia. I have included as well some East–West blends. The dishes are wholesome, sustaining, light and relatively easy to make. They may serve as starters, side dishes or complete meals in themselves. Make and savour them, and they will immediately become a regular part of your diet.

Although there are many types of pasta noodles found in China, Japan and Southeast Asia, not all of them are available in the West. Therefore, I have restricted myself to those which are dried and can be found in Chinese, oriental or Asian grocers. Some cannot be found in supermarkets but are easily obtained by mail-order (see page 187 for suppliers).

Below are some of the most common types of noodle available.

WHEAT NOODLES AND EGG NOODLES

These are made from hard or soft wheat flour and water. If egg has been added, the noodles are usually labelled as egg noodles. They can be bought dried or fresh from Chinese and oriental grocers, and many supermarkets and delicatessens also stock the dried variety. Flat noodles are usually used in soups, and rounded noodles are best for stir-frying. If you can't get Chinese noodles, you can use Italian egg noodles (dried or fresh) instead.

To cook wheat and egg noodles

Noodles are very good boiled and served instead of plain rice with main dishes. I think dried wheat or fresh egg noodles are best for this. If you are using fresh noodles, immerse them in a saucepan of boiling water and cook for 3–5 minutes or until they are soft. If you are using dried noodles, either cook them according to the instructions on the packet, or cook in boiling water for 4–5 minutes. Drain and serve.

If you are cooking noodles ahead of time before using them in another dish or before stir-frying them, toss the cooked drained noodles in a teaspoon or two of sesame oil and put them into a bowl. Cover this with cling film and put it in the refrigerator. The cooked noodles will remain usable for about 2 hours.

Udon

Udon are Japanese wheat noodles and can sometimes be found fresh at some supermarkets or Chinese or oriental grocers. Round or flat, they can be purchased dried and should be cooked until they are soft but not overcooked, so they still retain a little bite.

Buckwheat noodles

These Japanese noodles are thin and a brownish grey colour. Known as soba and extremely popular among the Japanese, they are often eaten as snacks, served cold in the summer and hot in the winter. They come fresh and dried, and can be found where Japanese food products are sold.

RICE NOODLES

Rice noodles are popular in southern China and throughout Southeast Asia. They are usually dried and can be found in Chinese and oriental grocers. Rice noodles are white and come in a variety of shapes. One of the most common is rice stick noodles, which are flat and about the length of a chopstick. They can also vary in thickness. Use the type called for in the recipe. Rice noodles are very easy to use. Simply soak them in warm water for 15 minutes or until they are soft. Drain them in a colander or sieve and they are then ready to be used in soups or to be stir-fried. Fresh rice noodles, which can also be found in Chinese and oriental grocers, are a popular type called 'fun noodles'. These need to be cooked straight away.

Fun rice noodles

The Chinese make large sheets of rice noodles from a basic mixture of rice flour, wheat *starch* (not flour) and water. This pasta is then steamed in sheets. When cooked, the sheets are cut into noodles to be eaten immediately. A very popular street snack in China, Hong Kong and Singapore, the fresh noodles are most often served with a sauce.

RICE PAPERS

Vietnamese rice papers are often beautifully textured by the imprint of the bamboo trays on which they are placed to dry. They are very thin dried sheets, usually round, and are used as wrappers for a Vietnamese-style spring roll. The dried sheets are very briefly soaked in water to soften them, then rolled around a filling and deep-fried to a light and crispy texture. Unlike the Chinese wrappers, the filled rice papers can be stored in the refrigerator for up to 3 hours before frying. Once they are fried, they can be kept crisp in a low oven for up to 2 hours.

BEAN THREAD (TRANSPARENT) NOODLES

These noodles, also called cellophane noodles, are made from ground mung beans and not from a grain flour. They are available dried, and are very fine and white. Easy to recognise packed in their neat, plastic-wrapped bundles, they are stocked by most Chinese grocers and some supermarkets. They are never served on their own, but are added to soups or braised dishes or are deep-fried as a garnish. They must be soaked in warm water for about 5 minutes before use. As they are rather long, you might find it easier to cut them into shorter lengths after soaking. They can also be fried, in which case do not soak them before using.

FRESH PASTA WITH CORIANDER, GINGER AND BASIL PESTO

This recipe was inspired by a colleague, Bruce Cost. A superb chef and author of excellent cookery books, one of his specialities is the food of Southeast Asia. Here, I elaborate on a version of his delicious Asian pesto. Pesto is an Italian term meaning any sauce whose ingredients have been pounded and mixed together. The original Genoan pesto sauce consists of fresh basil, Parmesan cheese, oil and garlic pounded into a smooth green paste. Ordinary fresh basil may be used here but, if you can, try to obtain the Asian tropical variety which has a distinctive basil-anise flavour worth savouring. Fresh coriander and ginger are, of course, traditional oriental seasonings. Combine this pesto with your own freshly made pasta, or buy dried or freshly made Chinese egg noodles.

Serves 6

10 oz (275 g) plain flour
3 large (size 1) eggs
2 tablespoons oil, preferably groundnut
1 teaspoon salt

Sauce
1 tablespoon finely chopped fresh ginger
1 tablespoon finely chopped fresh coriander
3 tablespoons finely chopped fresh basil
2 tablespoons finely chopped garlic
1 tablespoon oil, preferably groundnut
2 teaspoons sesame oil
2 teaspoons salt
1 teaspoon freshly ground black pepper

For the pasta, by hand or in a food processor, combine the flour, eggs, oil and salt. Knead the dough until smooth and satiny. Run the pasta through a pasta machine twice on each setting, stopping at the thinnest setting. Cut the pasta into thin noodles. Flour lightly and set aside.

Combine all the sauce ingredients and mix thoroughly in a blender. Set aside.

Bring a large saucepan of water to the boil. Add the pasta and cook for 1 minute. Drain thoroughly and toss with the sauce. Serve at once.

SPICY BEAN THREAD NOODLES WITH DRIED SHRIMPS
Photograph between pages 144 and 145

These noodles have a smooth, light texture that readily absorbs the surrounding flavours. In this recipe I follow my mother's example. Because most of the work involved can be done the day before and because the dish reheats so well, this may be called gourmet fast food. After a hard day's work, my mother preferred to serve a meal that was easily prepared yet full of flavour, and this was one of her favourites. The dried shrimps (page 24) may be found in most Chinese grocers and are very good, but they can be omitted. I include them to preserve the authenticity of the recipe. Take care when cooking the noodles because if they overcook they tend to lump together. Although the bean thread are known as noodles, this dish is delicious served with rice also.

Serves 2 to 4

1 oz (25 g) Chinese dried mushrooms, finely chopped
6 oz (175 g) bean thread (transparent) noodles
2 oz (50 g) dried shrimps
2 tablespoons oil, preferably groundnut
2 tablespoons finely chopped garlic
1 tablespoon finely chopped fresh ginger
2 tablespoons finely chopped shallots
2 teaspoons chilli bean sauce
2 teaspoons light soy sauce
2 teaspoons sugar
2 tablespoons rice wine or dry sherry
2 teaspoons chilli oil

Garnish
3 tablespoons finely chopped spring onions, green part only

Soak the dried mushrooms in warm water for 20 minutes. Drain them, squeeze out any excess liquid, cut off and discard the stalks and coarsely chop the mushrooms caps. Soak the noodles in a large bowl of warm water for 15 minutes. When soft, drain the noodles well. Cut into 3 inch (7.5 cm) lengths, using scissors or a knife. Soak the dried shrimps in a bowl of warm water for 15 minutes. When soft, drain the shrimps well.

Heat a wok or pan and add the oil. Put in the garlic, ginger, shallot and chilli bean sauce and stir-fry quickly for a few seconds. Add the shrimps, mushrooms and noodles and stir-fry for about 2 minutes. Stir in the soy sauce, sugar, rice wine and chilli oil and continue to cook the mixture over a gentle heat for about 5 minutes. Ladle the noodles into a large serving bowl, garnish with the spring onions and serve at once.

SPINACH AND RICE NOODLES

In this quick and healthy light meal, the dried noodles need only to be soaked and require very little cooking. Their texture is such that the spinach flavour, some of the colour and other seasonings are readily absorbed. Unlike egg noodles, rice noodles do not become sticky and gummy when they are moist; this makes it convenient to serve them cold. I add a little sugar to neutralise the iron and salt taste of the spinach.

Serves 2 to 4

$1\frac{1}{2}$ lb (700 g) fresh spinach
4 oz (110 g) rice noodles, rice vermicelli or rice sticks
1 tablespoon oil, preferably groundnut
2 teaspoons sugar
2 tablespoons coarsely chopped garlic
1 teaspoon salt
1 tablespoon light soy sauce
2 teaspoons chilli oil

Wash the spinach thoroughly. Remove all the stalks, leaving just the leaves.

Soak the rice noodles in a bowl of warm water for 25 minutes. Then drain them in a colander or sieve. (If you are using dried egg noodles, cook them for 3–5 minutes in boiling water, drain and immerse in cold water until required.)

Heat a wok or large pan to moderate heat and add the oil. Put in the salt and garlic and stir-fry for a few seconds. Add the spinach leaves and stir-fry for 2 minutes to coat the spinach leaves thoroughly. When the spinach has wilted to about a third of its original size, add the rice noodles, sugar, soy sauce and chilli oil, and continue to stir-fry for another 4 minutes. Transfer the noodles to a plate, and pour off any excess liquid. Serve hot or cold.

KOREAN BEAN THREAD SESAME NOODLES WITH VEGETABLES

Bean thread noodles are made from the starch of the mung bean and, when cooked, they are almost transparent. This simple to prepare recipe is my version of a popular Korean dish. What makes it memorable is the combination of lace-like noodles and exotic mushrooms, and unusual mixture of tastes and textures. The dried mushrooms and cloud ears are available at Chinese grocers and, because this is not an everyday dish, it is well worth the effort to obtain them.

Serves 4

1 oz (25 g) Chinese dried mushrooms
½ oz (10 g) Chinese dried cloud ears (black fungus)
4 oz (110 g) bean thread (transparent) noodles
2 oz (50 g) carrot
1 green pepper
1 small onion
2 tablespoons oil, preferably groundnut
4 fl oz (120 ml) water

Sauce
2 tablespoons light soy sauce
2 tablespoons dark soy sauce
3 tablespoons sesame oil
1½ tablespoons sesame seeds
1 tablespoon finely chopped garlic
1 tablespoon sugar
1 teaspoon freshly ground black pepper

Soak the dried mushrooms in warm water for 20 minutes until soft. Squeeze the excess liquid from the mushrooms and remove and discard the stalks. Cut the caps into shreds. Soak the cloud ears in warm water for about 20 minutes or until soft. Rinse them well in cold water and drain thoroughly in a colander.

Soak the noodles in a large bowl of very hot water for 15 minutes. When soft, drain well. Cut the noodles into 3 inch (7.5 cm) lengths, using scissors or a knife.

Peel and finely shred the carrot. Finely shred the pepper and onion.

Heat a wok or large frying-pan and add the oil. When moderately hot, add the mushrooms, cloud ears, carrot, onion, green pepper and water and stir-fry for 5 minutes or until the carrots are cooked.

Combine the sauce ingredients and add them to the vegetables. Give the mixture a good stir, then add the noodles. Stir-fry the mixture for 2 minutes until well heated through. Serve at once or at room temperature.

UDON NOODLES IN BROTH
Photograph between pages 144 and 145

During my student days I became a devotee of Japanese films, especially those that incidentally depicted scenes from daily life. Such films gave me insight into a culture that I had only read about and never directly experienced. Naturally, I was particularly interested in scenes showing eating habits and cookery. I noticed that the Japanese often seemed to be snacking on soup noodles, slurping them up and smacking their lips in a way that always made me hungry. I later learned that these were probably udon noodles, a Japanese favourite. Made from bleached white flour with no eggs, these noodles are very white and fine and vary in thickness. In an easy soup such as this, they make a hearty lunch.

Serves 4

12 oz (350 g) dried udon noodles (page 131)
8 oz (225 g) fresh or tinned tomatoes
8 spring onions
2 pints (1.1 ltr) chicken or vegetable stock
2 teaspoons salt
1 teaspoon freshly ground white pepper

Cook the noodles in a saucepan of boiling water for 4–5 minutes or according to the instructions on the packet. Drain the noodles, then put them into cold water until required.

If you are using fresh tomatoes, peel, seed and cut into 1 inch (2.5 cm) cubes. If you are using tinned tomatoes, chop them into small chunks. Cut the spring onions diagonally into 3 inch (7.5 cm) lengths.

Put the stock into a saucepan and bring to simmering point. Add the salt and pepper and simmer for 2 minutes. Stir in the noodles and tomatoes and simmer until heated through. Add the spring onions and simmer for a further 30 seconds, then serve.

CRISPY CANTONESE-STYLE NOODLES WITH VEGETABLES

The origins of pasta are obscured by time and controversy, but there is a general consensus that the Chinese first thought of the egg noodle variety. Whoever invented the process, pan-fried noodles make a perfect foundation for stir-fried dishes. Here, the pan-frying technique leaves the noodles brown, firm and crispy on the outside and yellow, moist and soft on the inside, a combination of textures that is classically Chinese. Upon this noodle base is placed a stir-fried vegetable topped with a zesty sauce.

Serves 2 to 4

1 oz (25 g) button mushrooms
6 spring onions
4 oz (110 g) red pepper
2 oz (50 g) celery
8 oz (225 g) dried or fresh thin Chinese egg noodles
2 tablespoons oil, preferably groundnut
4 garlic cloves, lightly crushed
4 oz (110 g) mange-tout, trimmed
2 teaspoons light soy sauce
2 tablespoons oyster sauce
2 teaspoons sugar
3 tablespoons rice wine or dry sherry
10 fl oz (300 ml) chicken or vegetable stock
2 teaspoons cornflour mixed with 2 teaspoons water

Finely shred the mushrooms, spring onions and pepper. Coarsely chop the celery.

If you are using dried noodles, cook them according to the instructions on the packet, otherwise boil for 2 minutes until soft. If you are using fresh Chinese noodles, boil for 3 minutes and then drain thoroughly. Scatter the noodles on a baking tray.

Heat a large frying-pan, preferably non-stick, and add 1 table-spoon of the oil. When hot, add the noodles and press down to make the noodles conform to the shape of the pan. Turn the heat to very low, and continue cooking for 10–15 minutes, until brown. Flip the noodles over in one piece and continue cooking them until the other side is brown. You may have to add a little oil or water from time to time to keep the noodles moist.

While the noodles are browning, heat a wok or large frying-pan until hot. Add the remaining oil and garlic and stir-fry for a few seconds. Put in the celery, mushrooms and pepper and stir-fry for 3 minutes. Add the mange-tout and spring onions and continue to stir-fry for another 2 minutes. Stir in the soy sauce, oyster sauce, sugar, rice wine and stock, and bring the mixture to the boil. Thicken with the blended cornflour until the sauce is cooked through.

Take out the noodles and place on a platter. Pour the vegetables and sauce over the noodles and serve at once.

TAN TAN NOODLES

To warm up on a cold afternoon or evening, serve Tan Tan noodles, which I first tasted in a Sichuan restaurant in Hong Kong. Given its Sichuan origin, I expected something spicy – but even so, I was quite unprepared for its explosive quality. The noodles arrived preceded by a wonderful aroma and were served in a bowl shimmering with red chilli oil. It was a delightful experience, featuring the classical spiciness of chilli beans, garlic, ginger and Sichuan preserved vegetable. I immediately tried to recreate the noodles when I returned home. The result is this recipe and I have enjoyed the noodles many times since. An essential ingredient is the Sichuan preserved cabbage or vegetable; it is worth the search and can be found in Chinese grocers. The dish can still be made if you omit it, but the Sichuan preserved cabbage elevates the dish far above the ordinary.

Serves 2

1 tablespoon oil, preferably groundnut
4 oz (110 g) Sichuan preserved cabbage or vegetable,
 rinsed and finely chopped
1 tablespoon finely chopped garlic
2 teaspoons finely chopped fresh ginger
2 tablespoons rice wine or dry sherry
1 tablespoon chilli bean sauce
1 tablespoon Chinese sesame paste or peanut butter
1 tablespoon dark soy sauce
1 tablespoon sugar
15 fl oz (400 ml) chicken or vegetable stock
8 oz (225 g) Chinese fresh or dried flat thin wheat or egg noodles

Heat a wok or large frying-pan over high heat and add the oil. Put in the preserved cabbage or vegetable, garlic and ginger and stir-fry for 1 minute. Add the rice wine, chilli bean sauce, sesame paste, soy sauce, sugar and stock. Reduce the heat and simmer for 3 minutes over low heat.

Bring a large pan of water to the boil and cook the noodles for 2 minutes if they are fresh and 5 minutes if dried. Drain well in a colander. Divide the noodles into individual bowls and ladle the sauce over them. Serve at once.

HOT AND SOUR NOODLES

Hot and sour is a popular combination in Chinese cookery. We Chinese love the two compatible tastes on our palate. This type of noodle dish is often served in snack noodle shops or food stalls in China and Hong Kong. It serves as a quick fast-food meal that is full of flavour and easily made. I prefer to eat it hot, but it is also good cold. This makes a speedy lunch dish.

Serves 2 to 4

1 lb (450 g) fresh or dried egg noodles
1 tablespoon sesame oil

Sauce
2 tablespoons dark soy sauce
1 tablespoon chilli oil
1 tablespoon Chinese black rice vinegar or cider vinegar
3 tablespoons finely chopped spring onions
¼ teaspoon freshly ground black pepper
1 teaspoon sugar

If you are using fresh noodles, cook first by boiling them for 3–5 minutes in a large saucepan of boiling water. If you are using dried noodles, cook in boiling water for 4–5 minutes. Drain the noodles, toss them in the sesame oil and then put aside until required.

Heat all the sauce ingredients in a small saucepan. Turn the heat down to low and simmer for 5 minutes.

Plunge the noodles into boiling water for 20 seconds, then drain them well in a colander or sieve. Quickly tip the noodles into a large bowl and pour the hot sauce over the top. Mix everything together well and serve at once.

SINGAPORE-STYLE RICE NOODLES

Rice noodles are lighter than wheat noodles and therefore lend themselves to dishes that are subtle and delicate. Singapore-style rice noodles are just such a treat. Whenever I visit Singapore or Hong Kong I sample this popular favourite, and I am never disappointed. The recipe traditionally includes tiny fresh shrimps and shredded ham and you may add some if you wish, but this recipe is appetising and pleasing vegetarian fare. The thin light noodles blend perfectly with the vegetables and curry sauce. This is equally delicious warm or cold, which makes it perfect for a picnic.

Serves 2 to 4

8 oz (225 g) rice noodles, rice vermicelli or rice sticks
4 oz (110 g) leeks
4 oz (110 g) carrots
4 oz (110 g) red peppers
4 spring onions
1 oz (25 g) fresh chillies
2 tablespoons oil, preferably groundnut
2 teaspoons salt
2 eggs, beaten
2 teaspoons sesame oil
$\frac{1}{2}$ teaspoon salt

Sauce
2 tablespoons curry paste
1 tablespoon finely chopped garlic
1 tablespoon finely chopped fresh ginger
10 fl oz (300 ml) chicken or vegetable stock
1 tablespoon sugar
2 tablespoons rice wine or dry sherry
2 tablespoons light soy sauce

Garnish
fresh coriander leaves

Soak the rice noodles in a bowl of warm water for 25 minutes. Drain in a colander or sieve. (If you are using dried egg noodles, cook for 3–5 minutes in boiling water, drain and immerse them in cold water until required.)

Wash and finely shred the white part of the leeks. Finely shred the carrots, peppers, spring onions and chilli. In a small bowl, combine the eggs with the sesame oil and salt.

Heat a wok or large pan over a high heat and add the oil. When almost smoking, add the carrots, leeks, spring onions and salt and stir-fry for a few seconds. Add the peppers and stir-fry for about 1 minute. Put in the curry sauce ingredients and the drained noodles. Stir-fry the mixture for about 5 minutes until well mixed and heated through. Then add the egg mixture, blending thoroughly. Stir-fry for 1 further minute. Serve at once, garnished with fresh coriander.

VEGETARIAN CHOW MEIN

Chow mein literally means 'stir-fried noodles'. It is a dish of universal popularity based upon its characteristic savoury combination of textures, tastes and colours whether made with meat or, as in this case, with vegetables. Chow mein can be kept warm for at least an hour without losing any of its charm; I enjoy it cold. Serve as an economical family meal or at a buffet party.

Serves 4

8 oz (225 g) fresh or dried egg noodles
2 oz (50 g) celery
2 oz (50 g) tinned bamboo shoots
2 tablespoons oil, preferably groundnut
3 garlic cloves, crushed
1 small onion, finely sliced
6 oz (175 g) small button mushrooms
1 tablespoon light soy sauce
2 tablespoons dark soy sauce
2 teaspoons finely chopped fresh ginger
3 tablespoons chicken or vegetable stock
1 tablespoon rice wine or dry sherry
1 teaspoon sugar
4 oz (110 g) bean sprouts

Garnish
fresh coriander sprigs

If you are using fresh noodles, blanch them first in a large pan of boiling water for 3–5 minutes. If you are using the dried noodles, cook in boiling water for 4–5 minutes. Drain the noodles, then put into cold water until required.

String the celery and slice diagonally. Shred the bamboo shoots.

Heat a wok or large frying-pan and add the oil. When moderately hot, add the garlic and stir-fry for 10 seconds. Add the onion, mushrooms, celery and bamboo shoots and stir-fry for about 5 minutes. Drain the noodles thoroughly and put into the wok. Continue to stir-fry for 1 minute, then add the rest of the ingredients, except the bean sprouts. Continue to stir-fry for another 2 minutes, then stir in the bean sprouts. Give the mixture a good stir and turn it onto a serving platter. Garnish with the fresh coriander sprigs.

LIGHT AND EASY RICE NOODLES

Making my way through the streets of Hong Kong and other Asian cities, I have often paused at kerbside food stalls to enjoy this 'fast food' dish. It is light but sustaining and easy to digest as you go about your business. This recipe makes a quick lunch for two using either fresh or dried flat rice noodles.

Serves 2

8 oz (225 g) dried flat rice noodles or
  $\frac{1}{2}$ recipe fresh rice 'fun' noodles (page 146)

Sauce
2 tablespoons hoisin sauce
$1\frac{1}{2}$ tablespoons light soy sauce
2 teaspoons chilli bean sauce
1 tablespoon sesame oil

Garnish
1 tablespoon toasted sesame seeds (page 23)

If you are using dried rice noodles, bring a large saucepan of water to the boil, remove it from the heat and add the rice noodles. Leave to stand for about 10 minutes, then drain thoroughly. If you are using fresh rice noodles, set up a steamer or fill a wok or deep casserole with at least 2 inches (5 cm) water. Put a rack into the wok or casserole and bring the water to the boil. Put the rice noodles onto a deep plate and lower the plate into the steamer or onto the rack. Cover the wok tightly. Gently steam on a low heat for 15–20 minutes.

Combine the sauce ingredients and pour over the softened or steamed noodles. Garnish with the sesame seeds and serve.

STIR-FRIED VEGETABLES OVER A RICE NOODLE CLOUD
Photograph overleaf

At Chinese banquets when I was a child, the food we children enjoyed most were the dishes that featured fried rice noodles. I believe this is still true today for Western children whose parents take them to Chinese restaurants. Practically any stir-fried dish with a little sauce makes a wonderful topping for these crisp, crackling, crunchy noodles. In this recipe, I combine them with slightly spiced vegetables, enhanced with aromatic seasonings.

Serves 4 to 6

10 fl oz (300 ml) oil, preferably groundnut, for deep-frying
6 oz (175 g) rice noodles, rice vermicelli or rice sticks
12 oz (350 g) aubergines
8 oz (225 g) courgettes
3 garlic cloves, crushed
4 spring onions, chopped
2 tablespoons rice wine or dry sherry
2 tablespoons yellow bean sauce
2 teaspoons chilli bean sauce
5 fl oz (150 ml) chicken or vegetable stock
1 teaspoon cornflour mixed with 1 teaspoon water
1 teaspoon sugar
2 tablespoons dark soy sauce
1 teaspoon salt

Heat the oil in a deep-fat fryer or large wok until very hot. Deep-fry the noodles until they are crisp and puffed up. Remove with a slotted spoon and drain on kitchen paper. You may have to do this in several batches.

Cut the aubergines and courgettes into 3 inch (7.5 cm) lengths. Sprinkle them with salt and leave in a sieve to drain for 20 minutes. Rinse under cold running water and pat dry with kitchen paper.

Opposite: *Vegetarian Dinner Party menu (page 186) including Bean Sprout Salad (page 78), Fragrant Coconut Rice (page 167), Asparagus with Tangy Mustard Dressing (page 80) and Braised Chinese Mushrooms (page 110)*
Overleaf: *Home-Made Chinese Rice 'Fun' Noodles with Peppers (page 148); Spicy Bean Thread Noodles with Dried Shrimps (page 134), Stir-Fried Vegetables over a Rice Noodle Cloud (above) and Udon Noodles in Broth (page 137)*

Heat a wok or large frying-pan and add $1\frac{1}{2}$ tablespoons of the oil in which you have fried the noodles. When moderately hot, add the garlic and spring onions and stir-fry for 30 seconds. Add the aubergines and courgettes and continue to stir-fry for 1 minute. Stir in the rest of the ingredients, except for the cornflour mixture, and cook for 3 minutes. Finally add the blended cornflour and cook for a further 1 minute.

Place the deep-fried noodles on a platter and spoon the vegetables over the top. Serve immediately.

SINGAPORE NOODLES

Singapore is a crossroads city in many ways, including the culinary. This delicious noodle recipe reflects just that, with its combination of Indian, Thai and Chinese influences. I enjoyed this dish during my first visit to Singapore, when it became an instant favourite. The noodles used were slightly thicker than the thin fresh egg noodles used here. They contrast perfectly with the fried beancurd cubes, and the finished dish makes a tempting meal for two.

Serves 2

8 oz (225 g) fresh or dried thin egg noodles
8 oz (225 g) firm beancurd
10 fl oz (300 ml) oil, preferably groundnut, for deep-frying
2 teaspoons oil, preferably groundnut
2 eggs, beaten
2 teaspoons sesame oil
$\frac{1}{2}$ teaspoon salt
2 tablespoons oil, preferably groundnut
2 garlic cloves, crushed
2 tablespoons light soy sauce
2 teaspoons chilli oil
3 tablespoons tomato purée
2 teaspoons sugar
2 tablespoons finely chopped spring onions
1 fresh chilli, seeded and shredded (optional)

Opposite: *Cold Honeydew Dessert Soup (page 174) and Rice Puffs with Prune Filling (page 180)*

If you are using fresh noodles, blanch them first by boiling for 3–5 minutes in a large saucepan of boiling water. If you are using dried noodles, cook in boiling water for 4–5 minutes. Drain the noodles, then put into cold water until required. Cut the beancurd into $\frac{1}{2}$ inch (1 cm) cubes.

Heat the 10 fl oz (300 ml) oil in a deep-fat fryer or a large wok until it almost smokes. Deep-fry the beancurd cubes for 1–2 minutes in 2 batches. When each batch of beancurd cubes is lightly browned, remove and drain well on kitchen paper.

Heat the 2 teaspoons of oil in a wok or frying-pan and add the eggs, sesame oil and salt. When cooked, the eggs should look like a thin, flat pancake. Remove from the pan, roll it up and cut in long 1 inch (2.5 cm) wide strips. Set aside.

Heat a wok or large frying-pan and add the 2 tablespoons of oil. When moderately hot, add the garlic and stir-fry for 30 seconds. Quickly drain the noodles and add them to the pan with the rest of the ingredients. Continue to stir-fry the noodles until all the ingredients are well mixed. Add the egg strips and beancurd and continue to stir-fry for another 3–4 minutes or until the beancurd is heated through.

HOME-MADE CHINESE FRESH RICE 'FUN' NOODLES

As a young apprentice working in my uncle's restaurant kitchen, I was always fascinated by his skill in making fresh rice noodles. He would make up the batter in the evening and then come in very early the next morning before the restaurant opened to steam the batter into noodles, using 5 enormous woks. I have never forgot being impressed by the way he managed to keep all the woks going at once, skipping quickly from one to the other. Freshly made rice noodles are very tasty, with a smooth, soft texture and a velvety surface that combines well with a light coating of sauce, as pasta should.

You should try making your own noodles a few times, if only to see if the freshly made ones really are superior to the packaged version. The rice flour and wheat starch (not the same thing as wheat flour) are readily available at Chinese grocers. The steaming technique assures a moist rice sheet that is easily rolled to be cut into noodles. Be sure to oil the steaming tin each time you add new batter, to prevent sticking. Once rolled and tightly wrapped, the sheets will keep in the refrigerator for at least 2 days, so you can cut the noodles just before you need to use them. Having mastered the technique and tasted the fresh noodles, I am sure you will make them often. Some Chinese grocers carry ready-made fresh 'fun' noodles.

Makes about 1 lb (450 g) fresh rice 'fun' noodles

8 oz (225 g) rice flour
6 tablespoons wheat starch
½ teaspoon salt
10 fl oz (300 ml) water
about 2 tablespoons oil, preferably groundnut
1 tablespoon sesame oil

In a large bowl, combine the rice flour, wheat starch, salt and water. Stir the batter until smooth and strain it through a fine sieve. Stir in the oil and sesame oil. Leave the batter to rest for 30 minutes.

Set up a steamer by adding 2 inches (5 cm) water to a wok or deep pan and bring to simmering point. Lightly oil a round baking tin which fits easily into the wok or pan.

Give the batter a good stir and add 5 or 6 tablespoons of the mixture to the baking tin. Gently tip it so that the batter coats the surface of the tin. Place the tin into the wok or pan so that it sits uncovered floating above the simmering water. Cover the wok tightly. Steam gently for 3–4 minutes or until the batter is cooked. Remove the baking tin and allow it to cool slightly. Gently roll up the rice sheet and repeat the process until all the batter is used up.

Cover the rolled up rice sheets with cling film and refrigerate for at least 1 hour before cutting. Cut the sheets into ½ inch (1 cm) wide noodles and use immediately. The 'fun' noodles can be steamed and then topped with a sauce or stir-fried.

HOME-MADE CHINESE RICE 'FUN' NOODLES WITH PEPPERS
Photograph between pages 144 and 145

Occasionally, on hot, humid Chicago summer evenings when my mother was understandably not in the mood for cooking, she would send me out to a local Chinese restaurant for some 'chow fun'. 'Fun' are freshly made soft, tender rice noodles which are usually combined with beef and bitter melon or beef and peppers. Either way, it was delicious. This is my vegetarian version of the dish and it is as much fun to prepare and to eat as the original. The texture of the noodles is a good contrast to that of the colourful, zesty peppers. Once the noodles are made, the rest is a simple stir-fry. Try adding chopped black beans as an experiment.

Serves 4

6 oz (175 g) yellow peppers
6 oz (175 g) red peppers
4 oz (110 g) green peppers
2 tablespoons oil, preferably groundnut
3 garlic cloves, crushed
1 lb (450 g) fresh 'fun' noodles (page 146)
1 tablespoon yellow bean sauce
2 tablespoons oyster sauce
1 tablespoon rice wine or dry sherry
2 tablespoons finely chopped spring onions
5 fl oz (150 ml) chicken or vegetable stock
1 teaspoon sugar

Cut the peppers into $\frac{1}{2}$ inch (1 cm) squares.

Heat a wok or large frying-pan and add the oil. When moderately hot, add the garlic and stir-fry for about 30 seconds. Add the noodles, peppers, yellow bean sauce, oyster sauce, rice wine, spring onions, stock and sugar, and stir-fry for about 3 minutes or until the peppers are thoroughly cooked. Turn out on a large serving platter and serve at once.

SEVEN

COLD PASTA & NOODLES

Chinese and Southeast Asian pasta is delicious hot or cold. When you make up the noodle dishes in this chapter, prepare them in basically the same way you would prepare hot noodles. The noodle recipes here are a sampling of my own favourite cold noodle delights. They are ideal for simple buffets and picnics and are more than merely adequate alternatives to hot pasta or noodle dishes.

I include here Spicy Black Bean Sauce Noodles and Cold Sichuan Noodles, which reflect the hot and spicy Chinese style, and Southeast Asian Noodle Salad and Cold Curry-Flavoured Noodles, which deliciously show the creativity of other regional styles. Because cold temperatures affect the potency of spices, it is best to experiment with these recipes to reflect your own personal preference.

COLD CHINESE NOODLE SALAD WITH MUSHROOMS

This is a simple dish that unites two satisfying foods, noodles and mushrooms, in a most appetising sauce. Hot oils are poured over ginger and spring onions, releasing their tangy flavours; the sauce is allowed to cool, then mixed with the noodles. The mushrooms are cooked separately to preserve their texture.

Serves 2

8 oz (225 g) fresh or dried thin Chinese egg noodles
1 tablespoon oil, preferably groundnut
2 garlic cloves, crushed
2 tablespoons rice wine or dry sherry
1 tablespoon light soy sauce
8 oz (225 g) small button mushrooms

Dressing
$\frac{1}{2}$ teaspoon freshly ground black pepper
3 tablespoons finely chopped spring onions
1 tablespoon finely chopped fresh ginger
$1\frac{1}{2}$ tablespoons light soy sauce
2 tablespoons oil, preferably groundnut
1 tablespoon sesame oil

If you are using fresh noodles, blanch first in a large saucepan of boiling water for 3–5 minutes. Immerse them in cold water. If you are using dried noodles, cook them in boiling water for 4–5 minutes. Drain the noodles, then put them into cold water until required.

Heat a wok or large frying-pan and add the oil. When moderately hot, add the garlic and stir-fry for 30 seconds. Stir in the rice wine, soy sauce and whole button mushrooms and stir-fry for 3 minutes or until the mushrooms are cooked. Remove from the pan and set aside. Wipe the wok clean.

Combine all the dressing ingredients, except the oils, in a small heatproof bowl. Reheat the wok and add both oils until they begin to smoke. Pour this mixture over the dressing ingredients in the bowl. Drain the noodles thoroughly in a colander. In a large bowl, combine the noodles, mushrooms and dressing. Mix well and serve immediately or within 3 hours.

CUCUMBER NOODLE SALAD

This is a simple vegetarian starter, ideal for warm weather meals. The bean thread noodles have a satiny smooth texture and their light flavour goes well with cucumbers, dressed in a piquant hot and sour sauce.

Serves 2

4 oz (110 g) bean thread (transparent) noodles
8 oz (225 g) cucumbers

Dressing
3 tablespoons light soy sauce
2 tablespoons Chinese white rice vinegar or cider vinegar
2 teaspoons chilli oil
1 tablespoon sugar
1 tablespoon oil, preferably groundnut
2 teaspoons finely chopped fresh ginger
3 tablespoons finely chopped spring onions

Soak the noodles in a large bowl of very hot water for 5 minutes. Drain and immerse them in cold water, then drain thoroughly in a colander. Cut the noodles into 3 inch (7.5 cm) lengths, using scissors or a knife.

Peel the cucumbers, slice them in half lengthways and, using a teaspoon, remove the seeds. Cut the cucumber halves into 3 inch (7.5 cm) lengths, $\frac{1}{4}$ inch (0.5 cm) thick.

In a large bowl, combine the dressing ingredients, then add the cucumbers and noodles. Mix thoroughly. Turn the salad onto a serving platter and serve immediately or within 3 hours.

SOUTHEAST ASIAN NOODLE SALAD
Photograph opposite page 112

On my first visit to Southeast Asia many years ago, what most impressed me was the use of exotic and fascinating combinations of ingredients such as coconut milk, limes, fish sauce and herbs such as basil, all of which were foreign to my tradition. I have since become familiar with these and other once strange ingredients, and my experiments have led me to some very delectable results, as with this light lunch or supper noodle dish, which includes an aromatic combination of splendid tastes and colours.

Serves 4

8 oz (225 g) flat rice noodles
2 spring onions
2 oz (50 g) mange-tout
2 oz (50 g) carrots
4 oz (110 g) bean sprouts

Dressing
2 tablespoons fresh lime juice
2 teaspoons chilli oil
$1\frac{1}{2}$ tablespoons light soy sauce
2 teaspoons sesame oil
1 tablespoon lemon juice
6 tablespoons fresh or tinned coconut milk (page 14)
$\frac{1}{2}$ teaspoon salt
grated rind of 1 lime
1 teaspoon fish sauce
$\frac{1}{2}$ teaspoon freshly ground black pepper
1 tablespoon sugar
2 tablespoons finely chopped fresh coriander
$1\frac{1}{2}$ tablespoons finely chopped fresh ginger
4 tablespoons finely chopped fresh basil

Garnish
3 tablespoons roasted peanuts, coarsely chopped

Bring a large saucepan of water to the boil, remove from the heat and add the rice noodles. Leave to stand for about 15 minutes, then drain and immerse them in cold water until required.

Finely shred the spring onions, mange-tout and carrots. Bring a pan of water to the boil and blanch the bean sprouts, spring onions, mange-tout and carrots for 1 minute. Immerse immediately in cold water, drain and set aside.

Combine all the ingredients for the dressing mixture. Drain the noodles thoroughly and toss them with the dressing mixture and the vegetables. Garnish with the peanuts and serve within 3 hours.

COLD CURRY-FLAVOURED NOODLES

Cold noodles can take strong flavours because the coldness mutes tastes. Here I have used Southeast Asian spices and seasonings and created a curry sauce strong enough to enliven the cold noodles. The sauce is cooked to bring out its full flavours, then cooled before mixing with the noodles. I like to serve these curried noodles with grilled meats; they also make a noteworthy side dish for many family meals.

Serves 2 to 4

1 lb (450 g) dried or fresh Chinese egg noodles

Dressing
1 tablespoon oil, preferably groundnut
2 tablespoons finely chopped garlic
1 tablespoon finely chopped onion
10 fl oz (300 ml) fresh or tinned coconut milk (page 14)
$\frac{1}{2}$ teaspoon turmeric
2 tablespoons curry paste
1 teaspoon salt
1 teaspoon sugar
2 tablespoons light soy sauce

Garnish
fresh basil or fresh coriander leaves

If you are using dried noodles, cook them according to the instructions on the packet or boil for 4–5 minutes. Immerse in cold water until required. If you are using fresh Chinese noodles, boil for 3–5 minutes, then cool them in cold water.

Heat a wok or pan and add the oil. When moderately hot, add the garlic and onion and stir-fry for 2 minutes. Stir in the coconut milk, turmeric, curry paste, salt, sugar and soy sauce and simmer for 4 minutes. Allow the dressing to cool.

Drain the noodles thoroughly and toss with the dressing. Turn onto a platter, garnish with the fresh herbs and serve within 3 hours.

SESAME BUCKWHEAT NOODLES

This simple dish is adapted from a traditional Japanese recipe. The buckwheat noodles have a unique texture that remains excellent when served cold. Perhaps this is because buckwheat, with a different structure from wheat or millet, is not a true cereal. I prefer to use thin buckwheat noodles for their lightness. This recipe will make a satisfying lunch for two.

Serves 2

1 lb (450 g) dried thin Japanese buckwheat soba noodles (page 131)

Dressing
1 tablespoon chilli oil
2 tablespoons sesame oil
1 tablespoon oil, preferably groundnut
3 tablespoons dashi (page 16) or chicken or vegetable stock
2 teaspoons sugar
2 tablespoons light soy sauce
½ teaspoon salt

Garnish
2 tablespoons toasted sesame seeds (page 23)
2 tablespoons spring onion tops, thinly diagonally sliced

Cook the dried noodles according to the instructions on the packet or boil for 4–5 minutes. Drain, then cool in cold water until required.

Combine the dressing ingredients together in a bowl. Drain the noodles thoroughly and toss them with the dressing. Garnish with the sesame seeds and spring onions and serve.

SPICY CITRUS-FLAVOURED NOODLES
Photograph opposite page 112

This versatile dish is perfect for warm weather eating, picnics, as a starter for an elegant dinner party or for large-scale entertaining. The egg noodles are a natural foil for the zest of the orange and lemon and combine perfectly with the spicy peanut sauce. Mix the noodles with the sauce *only* when you are about to serve the dish. If you prefer the sauce to be even spicier, simply add more chilli oil and garlic.

Serves 2 to 4

8 oz (225 g) dried or fresh Chinese egg noodles
1 tablespoon sesame oil

Sauce
1 dried red chilli
2 teaspoons oil, preferably groundnut
2 teaspoons sesame paste or peanut butter
2 tablespoons orange juice
2 teaspoons lemon juice
grated rind of 1 orange
grated rind of 1 lemon
1 teaspoon finely chopped spring onions
1 teaspoon finely chopped garlic
1 tablespoon Chinese white rice vinegar or cider vinegar
1 tablespoon dark soy sauce
2 teaspoons sugar
$\frac{1}{4}$ teaspoon Sichuan peppercorns
2 teaspoons chilli oil

If using dried noodles, cook them according to the packet instructions or boil for 4–5 minutes. Cool in cold water until required. If using fresh noodles, boil for 3–5 minutes, then immerse in cold water. In the same hot water, blanch the dried chilli until soft. Then blanch the lemon and orange rind for 30 seconds to remove their bitterness.

Mix the sauce ingredients together with the chilli in a bowl or in a blender. (This can be done in advance and kept refrigerated, as the sauce is served cold.)

Drain the cooked noodles, toss them with the sesame oil and arrange on a platter or in a large bowl. Toss the noodles well with the sauce just before serving.

FRAGRANT RICE NOODLE SALAD

This is a refreshing noodle salad from Southeast Asia. Although tomatoes are not indigenous to the region, oriental cooks have been completely won over since their introduction a century ago, and for good reason: they are flavoursome, colourful and nutritious. Except for the Eastern dressing ingredients, this could pass for a zesty Italian pasta dish.

Serves 2

8 oz (225 g) flat rice noodles
8 oz (225 g) tomatoes
2 oz (50 g) Italian (red) onions

Dressing
rind of 1 lime, finely chopped
2 tablespoons lime juice
2 tablespoons light soy sauce
1 tablespoon sugar
1 tablespoon oil, preferably groundnut
2 teaspoons finely chopped garlic
1 teaspoon chilli oil
1 teaspoon finely chopped fresh lemongrass
2 tablespoons finely chopped fresh coriander
2 tablespoons finely chopped fresh basil
1 tablespoon finely chopped fresh mint

Bring a large saucepan of water to the boil, remove from the heat and add the rice noodles. Leave to stand for about 15 minutes, then drain and immerse in cold water until required.

If you are using fresh tomatoes, peel, seed and coarsely chop. If you are using tinned tomatoes, coarsely chop. Finely slice the onions.

Combine all the dressing ingredients except for the fresh herbs. Thoroughly drain the noodles and toss them with the dressing, herbs, tomatoes and onions. Serve within 3 hours.

SPICY BLACK BEAN SAUCE NOODLES

Ever since I can remember, the aroma of black beans cooked with garlic has meant mouth-watering food. Because I enjoy cold noodles, I have adapted these seasonings for a light lunch dish or accompaniment for summer evening meals. The pungent sauce is cooked beforehand and allowed to cool before enlivening the cold noodles.

Serves 2

12 oz (350 g) fresh or dried Chinese egg noodles

Sauce
3 tablespoons oil, preferably groundnut
2 tablespoons yellow bean sauce
2 tablespoons black beans, coarsely chopped
2 tablespoons finely chopped garlic
1 tablespoon finely chopped fresh ginger
2 tablespoons finely chopped spring onions
2 teaspoons chilli bean sauce
2 teaspoons sugar
1 tablespoon dark soy sauce
2 teaspoons chilli oil
2 tablespoons rice wine or dry sherry
5 fl oz (150 ml) chicken or vegetable stock
1 teaspoon cornflour mixed with 1 teaspoon water

If you are using fresh noodles, blanch in a large saucepan of boiling water for 3–5 minutes, then immerse in cold water. If you are using dried noodles, cook in boiling water for 4–5 minutes. Drain the noodles, then put into cold water until required.

For the sauce, heat a wok or large frying-pan and add the oil. When moderately hot, add the yellow bean sauce, black bean sauce, garlic, ginger and spring onions and stir-fry for 2 minutes. Then add the rest of the ingredients, except the cornflour mixture, and continue to cook for 2 minutes. Stir in the blended cornflour and bring to the boil for 30 seconds. Remove from the heat and allow the sauce to cool. Drain the noodles thoroughly in a colander and mix with the sauce. Serve at once.

COLD SICHUAN NOODLES

In this Chinese recipe for spicy noodles, traditionally served hot, I have simply directed that it be eaten cold. This makes a delectable cold salad for warm weather days. It makes an ideal lunch dish for two, but the portions may be increased easily for use in a family meal.

Serves 2

1 lb (450 g) dried or fresh Chinese egg noodles
2 tablespoons oil, preferably groundnut
2 tablespoons finely chopped spring onions
1 tablespoon finely chopped garlic
1 tablespoon yellow bean sauce
2 teaspoons chilli bean sauce
2 teaspoons finely chopped fresh ginger
1 tablespoon rice wine or dry sherry
2 tablespoons dark soy sauce
2 tablespoons sesame oil

Garnish
fresh coriander leaves

If using dried noodles, cook them according to the packet instructions or boil for 4–5 minutes. Cool in cold water until required. If using fresh noodles, boil for 3–5 minutes, then immerse in cold water.

Heat a wok or large frying-pan and add the oil. When hot, add the spring onions, garlic, yellow bean sauce, chilli bean sauce and ginger and stir-fry for 2 minutes. Allow the mixture to cool thoroughly.

Drain the noodles and combine them with the cool seasonings, soy sauce and sesame oil. Garnish with coriander and serve within 3 hours.

EIGHT

RICE

Rice is the staple food of most of the Far East and Asia. Unlike bread, a Western staple that plays only a secondary role in Western cookery, rice is an integral part of every meal and is eaten many times during the day. Left-over rice is stir-fried or dried to use in rice cakes, simmered in a rice porridge, or simply eaten as a snack. Like beancurd, rice combines well with other foods and flavours. Somewhat bland by itself, it readily absorbs other tastes.

Each country treats rice in a different way, ranging from Thai Aromatic Fried Rice to the simple, austere Japanese Rice with Asparagus. Although there are numerous varieties of rice, for everyday use we need only be concerned with three: long-grain, short-grain and glutinous.

LONG-GRAIN RICE

This is the most popular rice for Asian food and is my own favourite, too. Although the Chinese still go through the ritual of washing it, I believe this step can be bypassed with rice purchased at supermarkets. Do not confuse it with the 'easy-cook' and other pre-cooked varieties which are widely available. They are unsuitable for the recipes in this book, except for those using coconut milk, which is rich in fats. It is worth trying to find the Thai aromatic long-grain rice, now available at many Chinese and oriental grocers. It has a pleasing fragrance similar to the basmati rice used in Indian cuisine.

To wash rice

This is an optional step. Put the required amount of rice into a large bowl, fill it with cold water and swish the rice around with your hands. Carefully pour off the cloudy water, keeping the rice in the bowl. Repeat this process several times until the water is clear.

To cook long-grain rice

These basic instructions for long-grain rice are given in my *Chinese Cookery* book. The method is easy and foolproof and always produces excellent results.

Fill a glass measuring jug with long-grain rice to the 15 fl oz (400 ml) level.

Put the rice into a large bowl and, if you wish, wash it in several changes of water until the water becomes clear. (This step may be omitted.) Drain the rice and put it into a heavy pan with $1\frac{1}{2}$ pints (900 ml) water and bring to the boil. Continue boiling until most of the surface liquid has evaporated. This should take about 15–

20 minutes. The surface of the rice should have small indentations like a pitted crater. At this point, cover the pan with a *very* tight-fitting lid, turn the heat as low as possible and let the rice cook undisturbed for 15–20 minutes. There is no need to 'fluff' the rice before serving it, but it should be thoroughly cooled before stir-frying.

A few rules are worth repeating in regard to long-grain rice:

■ The water should be at a level 1 inch (2.5 cm) above the surface of the rice; too much water means gummy rice. Recipes on commercial packets generally recommend too much water.

■ Never uncover the pan once the simmering process has begun; time the process and wait.

SHORT-GRAIN RICE

This rice is not to be confused with pudding rice. Short-grain rice, usually used in Chinese cooking for making porridge, is more popular in Japan. Varieties known as 'American Rose' or 'Japanese Rose' are quite suitable and can be found in many Chinese grocers or in shops that sell Japanese food products. Short-grain is slightly stickier than long-grain white rice, but is cooked in the same way (page 160) or can be steamed (page 162).

GLUTINOUS RICE

Glutinous rice is also known as sweet or sticky rice. It is short, round and pearl-like, and is not to be confused with ordinary short-grain or pudding rice. It has more gluten than ordinary rice, and when cooked is stickier and sweeter. It is used for substantial rice dishes such as Steamed Sticky Rice, or in stuffings, desserts and for making Chinese rice wine and vinegar. Most Chinese grocers stock it. Glutinous rice must be soaked for at least 2 hours (preferably overnight) before cooking. You may cook it in the same way as long-grain rice (page 160) or by steaming (page 162).

STEAMED STICKY RICE

In this recipe, the rice is suffused with many seasonings which are slowly steamed along with it. This is a dish my mother used to cook for me on those days when she could not be home to prepare lunch. She would make the dish and then set it in the warm steamer, where all the ingredients would slowly marry.

Serves 4

glutinous or short-grained rice to fill a measuring jug to 15 fl oz (400 ml) level
4 oz (110 g) dried shrimps (optional)
4 oz (110 g) fresh or frozen peas
4 oz (110 g) button mushrooms
1 tablespoon oil, preferably groundnut
1 tablespoon finely chopped fresh ginger
3 tablespoons finely chopped spring onions
2 tablespoons finely chopped Sichuan preserved vegetable
3 tablespoons rice wine or dry sherry
1 tablespoon oyster sauce
2 tablespoons light soy sauce

Put the rice in a large bowl, cover with water and leave to stand for 4 hours or overnight. Drain well. Set up a steamer or put a rack inside a wok or large, deep pan. Pour in about 2 inches (5 cm) water and bring it to the boil. Put the rice in a bowl and place this into the steamer or onto the rack. Cover the pan tightly, turn the heat low and steam gently for about 20 minutes.

If you are using dried shrimps, soak them in warm water for 20 minutes. Drain and discard the water. If you are using fresh peas, blanch in a pan of boiling water for 3 minutes; drain well. Immerse in cold water to stop them from cooking. Finely slice the mushrooms.

Heat a wok or large frying-pan and add the oil. When moderately hot, add the oil, ginger, spring onions and shrimps and stir-fry for 2 minutes. Add the mushrooms and Sichuan preserved vegetables and continue to cook for 5 minutes or until most of the liquid has evaporated. Add the rice wine, oyster sauce and soy sauce and continue to cook for 2 minutes. Stir in the steamed rice and peas.

Replenish the steamer with hot water. Transfer the rice mixture into a bowl and steam for another 30 minutes over low heat. It is now ready to be served. This rice can be kept warm in the steamer, with the heat turned off, for 25 minutes. It also reheats well.

THAI AROMATIC FRIED RICE

Thai cuisine has been influenced by the Chinese, but there is a great deal of originality in the Thai tradition. This recipe is distinctly Thai, as the combination of fish sauce and chilli bean sauce is not normally used with rice in Chinese cookery. The pungent flavour of the fish sauce mellows when it is cooked, leaving a fragrant aroma. The result is an unusually piquant rice dish. You may stir-fry the cooked rice without waiting for it to cool.

Serves 4

2 tablespoons oil, preferably groundnut
4 oz (110 g) onion, finely chopped
long-grain rice measured to the 15 fl oz (400 ml) level
    in a measuring jug and cooked (page 160)
$\frac{1}{4}$ teaspoon salt
1 tablespoon fish sauce
2 teaspoons chilli bean sauce
3 tablespoons tomato purée
3 tablespoons finely chopped spring onions
2 tablespoons finely chopped fresh coriander
4 eggs, beaten

Heat a wok or large frying-pan and add the oil. When moderately hot, add the onion and stir-fry for 3 minutes. Put in the rice and continue to stir-fry for another 3 minutes. Add the rest of the ingredients, except the eggs. Stir-fry the mixture for a further 5 minutes over a high heat. Next add the beaten eggs and cook for 3 minutes or until the eggs have set. Turn the mixture onto a platter and serve.

SWEETCORN AND GINGER FRIED RICE

Sweetcorn and rice go well together, with their contrasting and complementary textures, colours and flavours. The addition of ginger makes them a little exotic – a true East–West delight. Use fresh corn if possible, and be sure the cooked rice is cold before stir-frying. This will keep it from absorbing too much oil and becoming sticky. This economical and healthy dish may be eaten as a rice salad or vegetable accompaniment to other foods.

Serves 4

1 lb (450 g) fresh sweetcorn on the cob, or 10 oz (275 g) tinned sweetcorn
1 tablespoon oil, preferably groundnut
1½ tablespoons finely chopped fresh ginger
2 tablespoons finely chopped spring onions
2 tablespoons rice wine or dry sherry
long-grain rice measured to the 15 fl oz (400 ml) level
   in a measuring jug and cooked (page 160)
¼ teaspoon salt
¼ teaspoon freshly ground pepper
2 tablespoons sesame oil

Remove the corn kernels with a sharp knife or cleaver. You should end up with about 10 oz (275 g). If you are using tinned corn, empty the contents into a sieve, drain well and set aside.

Heat a wok or large frying-pan until hot and add the oil. Put in the ginger and spring onions and stir-fry for a few seconds. Add the rice wine and continue to stir-fry a few more seconds. Stir in the cold cooked rice and stir-fry for 5 minutes, then add the corn, salt and pepper, and continue to stir-fry for 2 minutes. Finally, add the sesame oil and stir-fry for a further 4 minutes until the corn is thoroughly cooked. Serve at once, or cold as a rice salad.

HONG KONG-STYLE FRIED RICE

One of the many memorable meals I have enjoyed in Hong Kong included a dish of rice, stir-fried with Chinese broccoli stalks and eggs. I first sampled it in the delightful company of the eminent food critic Willie Mark, who guided me to the restaurant that served it. Ordinary broccoli (calabrese) also works well in this recipe.

Serves 4

2 tablespoons oil, preferably groundnut
8 oz (225 g) fresh broccoli or Chinese broccoli
4 oz (110 g) fresh or frozen peas
1 teaspoon salt
2 tablespoons water
long-grain rice measured to the 15 fl oz (400 ml) level
   in a measuring jug and cooked (page 160)
2 eggs, beaten
2 teaspoons sesame oil

Separate the broccoli heads into florets. Peel the stalks if necessary, then slice. Dice the broccoli into very small pieces.

If you are using fresh peas, blanch in a small saucepan of boiling water for 2 minutes; if using frozen peas, blanch for 1 minute.

Heat a wok or large frying-pan and add the oil. When moderately hot, add the broccoli, peas and salt and stir-fry for about 1 minute, then add the water. Continue to stir-fry the mixture for about 2 minutes or until the broccoli is cooked. Add the cold cooked rice and stir-fry for 3 minutes. Then add the eggs and sesame oil and stir-fry for a further 2 minutes. Turn the mixture onto a platter and serve at once.

CHINESE RICE PORRIDGE WITH CONDIMENTS

Porridge in the West is a plain yet sustaining dish; in Eastern cookery, porridge is soothing, warm and aromatic. Chinese porridge is usually quite tasty, depending on the flavourings added, and Malaysian porridge is always fiery. This stimulating lunch dish is based upon Malaysian porridge, the seasonings being typical of this cuisine. I like to place the garnish around the porridge before stirring it in because it looks so attractive.

Serves 2

2 pints (1.1 ltr) chicken or vegetable stock
short-grain rice to fill a glass measuring jug to 15 fl oz (400 ml) level
2 teaspoons salt

Garnish
1 garlic clove
2 spring onions
1 fresh chilli
1 tablespoon finely chopped fresh coriander
1 tablespoon light soy sauce
1 egg
1 teaspoon chilli oil
4 oz (110 g) fresh or tinned tomatoes, chopped
1 oz (25 g) roasted peanuts

Bring the stock to the boil in a large saucepan and add the rice and salt. Return the mixture to the boil and give it several good stirs. Turn the heat down to low and cover the pan. Simmer for about

45 minutes, stirring occasionally to keep it from sticking.

For the garnish, finely shred the garlic, spring onions and chilli. Arrange the garnishes on a separate platter. When you are ready to serve the porridge, add the garnishes and serve at once.

PINEAPPLE FRIED RICE
Photograph opposite page 113

I first enjoyed this unusual rice dish in Hong Kong and only subsequently learned that it is of Thai origin. Thai cooks commonly hollow out the pineapple and fill it with fried rice or some other tasty stuffing. It is a very attractive way to serve fried rice, but hollowing out the fruit takes a little effort and is not to be done every day. An easier alternative is to cut the pineapple in half lengthways. This attractive dish makes an impressive centrepiece for a special dinner party.

Serves 4 to 6

1 large fresh pineapple
1 oz (25 g) Chinese dried mushrooms
2 tablespoons oil, preferably groundnut
1 small onion, finely chopped
4 oz (110 g) Chinese long beans, runner beans or French beans,
* trimmed and diced*
long-grain rice measured to the 15 fl oz (400 ml) level
* in a measuring jug and cooked (page 160)*
2 eggs
2 tablespoons dark soy sauce
1 tablespoon fish sauce

Carefully cut off and save the pineapple top, leaving about 1 inch (2.5 cm) of the pineapple under the leaves, if you want to use the whole shell for serving. Alternatively, you can cut the pineapple in half lengthways after disposing of the top and leaves. Scoop out the inside fruit, leaving the outer shell of the pineapple intact to serve the fried rice. Coarsely chop the pineapple flesh, discarding the tough centre core.

Soak the dried mushrooms in warm water for 20 minutes until soft. Squeeze out the excess liquid from the mushrooms and remove and discard the stalks. Cut the caps into small dice.

Heat a wok or large frying-pan and add the oil. When almost smoking, add the mushrooms, onions and beans and stir-fry for 1 minute. Mix in the cold cooked rice and stir-fry for 1 minute. Add the eggs, soy sauce and fish sauce and continue to stir-fry for 5 minutes over high heat. Stir in the chopped pineapple and stir-fry for about 2 minutes. Spoon the mixture into the hollowed-out pineapple shell and replace the top, or pile the mixture onto the two halves, and serve the remaining rice on a platter.

FRAGRANT COCONUT RICE
Photograph opposite page 113 and opposite page 144

For this recipe you may use 'easy-cook' rice. It is one of those rare dishes in which such pre-cooked rice works well, partly because of the richness and oils in the coconut. Unusual as the combination of spices may seem, you will find them a harmonious blend with this dish. If you use long-grain rice it will be a little sticky, as it should be. The rice reheats well but should be warmed over a very low heat.

Serves 4

2 tablespoons oil, preferably groundnut
6 oz (175 g) finely chopped onion
long-grain or 'easy cook' rice measured to the 15 fl oz (400 ml) level
 in a measuring jug
1 teaspoon turmeric
2 teaspoons salt
15 fl oz (400 ml) fresh or tinned coconut milk (page 14)
5 fl oz (150 ml) chicken or vegetable stock
2 whole cloves
1 whole cinnamon stick or Chinese cinnamon bark
2 bay leaves

Heat the oil in a large flameproof casserole until moderately hot. Add the onion and stir-fry for 2 minutes. Put in the rice, turmeric and salt, and continue to cook for 2 minutes.

Add the coconut milk and stock and bring the mixture to the boil. Stir in the whole cloves, cinnamon and bay leaves. Turn the heat as low as possible and cook the rice undisturbed for 20 minutes. It is ready to serve when the rice is cooked.

JAPANESE RICE WITH ASPARAGUS

This is a traditional Japanese dish, classic in its simplicity. Appealing to the eye as well as the palate, it is so satisfying that it is almost a meal in itself. This delectable dish is based on short-grain rice. You can substitute broccoli or runner beans for the asparagus.

Serves 2 to 4

short-grain rice measured to the 15 fl oz (400 ml) level in a measuring jug
1¼ pints (700 ml) chicken or vegetable stock
2 tablespoons light soy sauce
1 tablespoon dark soy sauce
5 fl oz (150 ml) sake, rice wine or dry sherry
1 lb (450 g) fresh asparagus
2 tablespoons oil, preferably groundnut
¼ teaspoon salt
2 tablespoons finely shredded fresh ginger

Cook the rice according to the method given for long-grain rice on page 160, but substitute stock for the water and add the soy sauce and sake.

Cut off the tough ends of the asparagus, then cut the stalks diagonally into 3 inch (7.5 cm) long pieces.

Heat a wok or large frying-pan and add the oil. Put in the asparagus pieces and salt and stir-fry for 4 minutes. Remove the asparagus from the pan and leave to cool.

Fold the asparagus and ginger into the warm cooked rice and serve.

TWO-MUSHROOM RICE

This is a simple vegetarian adaptation of a traditional chicken-rice-mushroom dish my mother often made when I was a child. Even without the chicken, it remains a favourite of mine. One must properly appreciate the mushroom which, in the words of a discriminating scholar, 'belongs to that category of plants used in cooking whose main function is to add less flavour than the spices and herbs, less bulk than the real vegetables, and to absorb differentially the flavours of the dish, in order to bring out, by subtle chemistry, the highest and most delicate tastes'. Once you begin to think of mushrooms in this way and to use them accordingly, all mushroom dishes take on a special charm and flavour. Save the water in which the dried mushrooms have been soaked, as they give an additional earthy flavour to the cooked rice.

Serves 4

1 oz (25 g) Chinese dried mushrooms
1½ pints (900 ml) very hot water
8 oz (225 g) button mushrooms
1 tablespoon oil, preferably groundnut
3 tablespoons finely chopped spring onions
½ teaspoon salt
2 tablespoons light soy sauce
long-grain rice measured to the 15 fl oz (400 ml) level
* in a measuring jug*

Soak the dried mushrooms in 1½ pints (900 ml) very hot water for 20 minutes until soft. Remove them with a slotted spoon and save the liquid. Squeeze the excess liquid from the mushrooms and remove and discard the stalks. Cut the caps into quarters. Cut the button mushrooms into quarters.

Heat a wok or large frying-pan and add the oil. When hot, add the spring onions, salt and button mushrooms and stir-fry for 2 minutes. Put in the dried mushrooms and stir-fry for another minute or until all the liquid has evaporated. Remove the mixture and set aside.

Add the mushrooms, soy sauce and mushroom liquid to the rice in a pan and bring it to the boil. Continue boiling until most of the surface liquid has evaporated. This should take about 15–20 minutes. At this point, cover the pan with a very tight-fitting lid, turn the heat as low as possible and let the rice cook undisturbed with the mushrooms for 15–20 minutes.

CURRIED FRIED RICE WITH GREEN BEANS

Curried rice has an appealing and exotic aroma, and beans add colour and a contrast of textures. An exception to the classic rule for stir-frying rice, this cooked rice may be stir-fried immediately, without waiting for it to cool. This is a grand rice dish for any meal.

Serves 4

2 tablespoons oil, preferably groundnut
4 oz (110 g) Chinese long beans, runner beans or French beans, trimmed and diced
long-grain rice measured to the 15 fl oz (400 ml) level in a measuring jug and cooked (page 160)
1 tablespoon finely chopped garlic
3 tablespoons finely chopped fresh coriander
grated rind of $\frac{1}{2}$ lime
2 dried chillies, seeded and chopped
2 tablespoons fish sauce
2 teaspoons sugar
2 tablespoons curry paste
$\frac{1}{2}$ teaspoon salt

Heat a wok or large frying-pan and add the oil. When moderately hot, add the beans and stir-fry for about 2 minutes. Put in the rice and continue to stir-fry for 3 minutes. Stir in the rest of the ingredients and mix thoroughly. Cook for a further 5 minutes, stirring continuously. Turn the mixture onto a plate and serve at once.

SINGAPORE-STYLE LETTUCE FRIED RICE

This is an easy fried rice dish to make. The chilli adds zest and sparkle to the dish, and the lettuce provides a refreshing touch.

Serves 4

$\frac{1}{2}$ oz (10 g) Chinese dried mushrooms
2 tablespoons oil, preferably groundnut
4 shallots, sliced
3 garlic cloves, crushed
long-grain rice measured to the 15 fl oz (400 ml) level
    in a measuring jug and cooked (page 160)
2 oz (50 g) fresh or frozen peas
3 tablespoons finely chopped spring onions
2 fresh chillies
2 eggs, beaten
3 tablespoons light soy sauce
$\frac{1}{2}$ teaspoon salt
$\frac{1}{4}$ teaspoon freshly ground black pepper
8 oz (225 g) iceberg lettuce, finely shredded

Garnish
2 tablespoons finely chopped spring onions

Soak the dried mushrooms in warm water for 20 minutes until soft. Squeeze the excess liquid from the mushrooms and remove and discard the stalks. Cut the caps into small dice.

Heat a wok or large frying-pan and add the oil. When almost smoking, add the shallots and garlic and stir-fry for 30 seconds. Put in the cold cooked rice and stir-fry for 1 minute, then add the peas, spring onions and chillies and continue to stir-fry for another 3 minutes. Stir in the beaten egg, soy sauce, salt and pepper and stir-fry for a further 2 minutes or until the eggs have set.

Finally, add the lettuce and mix thoroughly. Turn the mixture onto a serving plate and garnish with the spring onions. Serve at once.

NINE

DESSERTS

Chinese, Japanese and Southeast Asian cookery is known through-out the world for its rich variety and savoury tastes rather than for its desserts. Many tend to be oversweet, heavy and rather unappealing to the Western palate. I think fresh fruit in season is generally the best dessert to serve after the subtle richness of this cuisine, but in this short chapter are several more traditional desserts, some based on fruit or delicate egg custard, and including chewy rice balls and sweet crunchy wuntuns.

COLD HONEYDEW DESSERT SOUP
Photograph opposite page 145

I first sampled this delicious dessert at the Sichuan Garden Res-taurant in Hong Kong. It is suffused with the tastes, fragrances, textures and colours popular in Southeast Asia. While in the West we tend to prefer the firm white flesh of mature coconuts, in Southeast Asia the slightly green or immature coconut is preferred. The flesh is quite soft, like a jelly, and can be scooped out with a spoon or one's fingers. The liquid from such coconuts is also rather sweet. Mature coconuts are sweet too, especially when combined with milk and melon. The tapioca adds body to the soup, and the result is an unusually refreshing dessert, perfect after any meal.

Serves 6 to 8

4 tablespoons small pearl tapioca
5 fl oz (150 ml) water
1 ripe honeydew melon, about 4 lb (1.8 kg)
1¼ pints (700 ml) fresh or tinned coconut milk (page 14)
6 tablespoons sugar

Combine the tapioca and water in a small bowl and leave to stand for 45 minutes.

Cut the honeydew melon into quarters, remove the seeds and cut off the peel. Cut the melon into large pieces. Purée the flesh in a blender to a thick liquid consistency. Pour into a medium-sized bowl and refrigerate.

Place the coconut milk in a saucepan, add the sugar and tapioca and simmer for 5 minutes or until it thickens. Allow it to cool, then refrigerate.

When you are ready to serve the soup, pour the two separate mixtures into a large serving bowl, stir well and serve.

SWEET GINGER CUSTARD

This creamy smooth and light custard is enlivened by the zest of preserved ginger. This is, in fact, a blend of East and West that works very well. It can be served warm or cold and is a delightful finish to any meal. Make this custard in great quantities because it retains its flavours nicely and one never tires of it. Do not use the Chinese preserved ginger sold in jars with syrup, as it is too strong for this recipe and will overpower the custard.

Serves 10

2 vanilla pods
4 oz (110 g) sugar
1 pint (570 ml) low-fat milk
6 large (size 1) eggs, beaten
2 tablespoons finely chopped preserved ginger

Split the vanilla pods in half and scrape out the seeds with a spoon. Separate the seeds with 1 tablespoon of the sugar and set to one side.

Preheat the oven to Gas Mark 6, 400°F (200°C). Combine the milk, vanilla pods and ginger in a pan and leave it to heat gently. Meanwhile, whisk the eggs, sugar and vanilla seeds in a large bowl. Then, when the milk is steaming hot, discard the vanilla pods and pour the milk into the egg and sugar mixture in a slow and steady stream, whisking until thoroughly blended.

Pour the liquid into a gratin dish and place it in a large roasting tin. Transfer the tin carefully to the oven, then pour in sufficient hot water to come two-thirds up the sides of the dish. Turn the temperature down to Gas Mark 4, 350°F (180°C) and bake for 45 minutes or until done. Serve warm, or cool to room temperature before refrigerating.

BANANA CRISPS

This is a popular Thai dessert or snack. The bananas must be sliced very thinly by hand, not with a food processor. Buy the firmest ones you can find. Indonesians normally use green, underripe bananas, which are easier to slice. Remember that the crisps continue to cook after being removed from the oil, so you must not leave them in for too long. The sugar in the bananas caramelises as they cool. Your touch with this recipe will improve as you master the method. Once the fried banana slices have cooled thoroughly, they become quite crispy. Serve warm or cold.

Serves 4

3 firm bananas
15 fl oz (400 ml) oil, preferably groundnut, for deep-frying
caster or icing sugar, for dusting

Peel and slice the bananas into very thin rounds.

Heat the oil in a deep-fat fryer or wok until hot. Fry several slices of the banana at a time for 2–3 minutes, or until they are a deep golden brown, taking care not to burn them. Drain on kitchen paper and allow to cool. Dust them lightly with sugar and serve.

CHINESE TOFFEE APPLES

There are many versions of this well-known Chinese dessert. I like this one, which I learned in Hong Kong, because it is easy to make. Instead of having to prepare a batter, the apples are simply rolled in cornflour. Some dexterity is required, but that will come with practice, and these apples are so good you will find yourself practising a great deal. I would suggest making it for family consumption a few times before trying it for special guests.

Serves 4

2 medium firm eating apples
juice from 1 lemon
2 oz (50 g) cornflour
15 fl oz (400 ml) oil, preferably groundnut, for deep-frying
8 oz (225 g) sugar
15 fl oz (400 ml) water
2 tablespoons white sesame seeds
iced water

Peel and core the apples and cut each into 8 large wedges. Mix with the lemon juice to prevent them from browning. Sprinkle the apple wedges with the cornflour until well coated.

Heat the oil in a deep-fat fryer or wok until moderately hot. Lift out several pieces of apple at a time and shake off any excess cornflour. Deep-fry for 2 minutes or until golden. Remove with a slotted spoon and drain on kitchen paper. Repeat the process until you have deep-fried all the apple wedges.

Combine the sugar and water in a pan. Heat the mixture until the sugar melts and begins to caramelise. Turn the heat to *very* low and watch carefully to prevent the syrup from burning. Add the sesame seeds.

Just before serving, prepare a bowl of iced water filled with ice cubes. Reheat the oil to moderate and deep-fry the apples a second time for about 2 minutes. Drain again on kitchen paper. Gently add the fried apples to the caramel syrup to coat. Remove with a slotted spoon and put the coated apple pieces into the iced water to harden. Do a few at a time to prevent them from sticking together. Remove from the water and place on a serving platter. Serve at once.

INDONESIAN FRIED BANANAS

This naturally sweet and flavoursome dessert is based on an Indonesian recipe but is actually a common treat all over Southeast Asia. It is easy to make and the number of portions may be doubled or trebled.

Serves 2

3 ripe bananas
2 oz (50 g) plain flour
2 tablespoons sugar
1 egg, beaten
5 fl oz (150 ml) water
15 fl oz (400 ml) oil, preferably groundnut, for deep-frying
caster or icing sugar, for dusting

Peel the bananas and cut them in half widthwise. For the batter, combine the flour, sugar, egg and water in a small bowl. Mix well to form a smooth, thick batter.

Heat the oil in a deep-fat fryer or wok until moderately hot. Put the banana halves into the batter mixture, then lift out the fruit using a slotted spoon and drain off any excess batter. Deep-fry each piece for about 2 minutes until golden and crispy. Remove with a slotted spoon and drain on kitchen paper. Repeat the process until you have fried all the bananas. Arrange them on a serving platter and dust with sugar. Serve at once.

SWEET WUNTUNS

In China, these wuntuns are called firecrackers because of their shape. This recipe is my variation on that popular Chinese theme. Instead of the traditional stuffing of dates, I use sultanas or raisins combined with desiccated coconut and walnuts. The result is a sweet, crunchy and delectable dessert. They may be cooked hours in advance but are tastiest when eaten warm. These wuntuns are quite addictive; try them just with tea.

Makes about 30–35 wuntuns

1 packet wuntun skins (about 30–35 skins)
1 pint (570 ml) oil, preferably groundnut, for deep-frying
icing sugar for dusting

Filling
4 oz (110 g) sultanas or raisins
2 oz (50 g) desiccated coconut
3 oz (75 g) walnuts, shelled
1 oz (25 g) sugar
grated rind of 1 lemon
1 egg, beaten

Combine the filling ingredients together in a large bowl and mix well. Then, using a teaspoon, put a small amount of filling in the corner of each wuntun skin. Roll it diagonally halfway to the centre, pinch down the sides around the filling, wet the corner

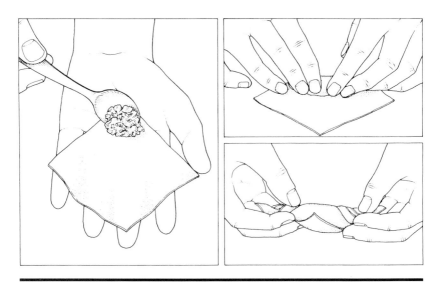

with water and fold over to seal well. Gently twist the ends to make an attractive decorative package like a firecracker.

Heat the oil in a deep-fat fryer or large wok until hot. Deep-fry the filled wuntuns in several batches until they are golden brown, about 3–5 minutes. Remove the cooked wuntuns with a slotted spoon and drain on kitchen paper. Dust lightly with the icing sugar and serve warm or at room temperature.

MALAYSIAN COCONUT CUSTARD

Custards are well known around the world, but coconut custard is specifically Thai and Malaysian in origin. In these countries it is usually steamed, but I find it even better cooked in the traditional Western manner, in a hot water bath in the oven. The rich coconut flavour permeates the custard, making it a perfect dessert served hot or cold. Make it in individual 4 oz (110g) ramekins if you can.

Serves 6 to 8

4 eggs, beaten
4 oz (110 g) sugar
15 fl oz (400 ml) fresh or tinned coconut milk (page 14)
$\frac{1}{4}$ teaspoon salt

Decoration
4 oz (110 g) desiccated coconut

Combine the eggs, sugar, coconut milk and salt in a large bowl and mix well.

Preheat the oven to Gas Mark 2, 300°F (150°C).

Pour the custard mixture into individual ramekins or a large baking dish. Place the ramekins or dish inside a large roasting tin. Transfer the tin carefully to the oven, then pour in sufficient hot water to come two-thirds up the sides of the dishes or dish. Bake for 35 minutes if you are using ramekins, or 1 hour if you are using a large baking dish. You can test if the custard is done by inserting the blade of a knife into the centre of the custard. When the custard is done, the blade will come out clean.

Cool and chill the custard until you are ready to serve it. Lightly brown the coconut in a frying-pan over moderate heat. Allow it to cool, sprinkle over the top of the custard and serve.

RICE PUFFS WITH PRUNE FILLING
Photograph opposite page 145

These sweet rice balls are a satisfying snack or dessert. They were a favourite treat when I was a boy, with their chewy texture and sweet centre. My mother made them with a filling of sweet bean paste, but I find that prunes are just as satisfying. The rice balls will puff up and split slightly as they are heated, but don't worry as they will still retain their shape and centres.

Makes about 14 rice balls

8 oz (225 g) glutinous rice flour
10 fl oz (300 ml) hot water
14 prunes
3 tablespoons white sesame seeds
15 fl oz (400 ml) oil, preferably groundnut, for deep-frying

First make the dough. Put the rice flour in a large bowl and gradually stir in the hot water, mixing it all the while with a fork or with chopsticks until most of the water is incorporated. The mixture will be quite sticky. Remove the mixture from the bowl and knead it with your hands until smooth, dusting it from time to time to keep the dough from sticking. This should take about 5–6 minutes. Put the dough back into the bowl, cover it with a clean, dry tea towel, and leave to rest for about 30 minutes.

While the dough is resting, stone the prunes.

After the resting period, take the dough out of the bowl and knead it again for about 2 minutes, dusting it with a little rice flour if sticky. Once the dough is smooth, form it into a roll about 9 inches (25 cm) long and about 1 inch (2.5 cm) in diameter. Take a knife and cut the roll into about 14 equal pieces.

Roll each of the dough pieces into a small round pancake about 3 inches (7.5 cm) in diameter. Put a prune in the centre of each pancake and bring up the sides pinching the edges to seal well. Roll it into a ball and sprinkle with sesame seeds. Transfer the finished balls to a floured tray and keep them covered until you have filled all the balls in this way.

Heat the oil in a deep-fat fryer or wok until hot. Deep-fry the rice balls in several batches until golden, about 5 minutes. The rice balls will puff up and they may split slightly, popping and splattering fat, so stand well back. Remove with a slotted spoon and drain them on kitchen paper. Serve at once.

SUGGESTED MENUS

The following ten menu suggestions are simply a guide to get you started, as the recipes in this book are very versatile and can be combined in many different ways for lunches, suppers and hearty dinners, or for picnics or buffet parties. Use your imagination to create your own menus, and feel free to mix oriental dishes with Western food to make the most of both traditions. Check the number of servings yielded by each individual recipe and adjust the amounts as required to suit the number of people you are catering for, taking into account the number of other dishes you will be providing at the same meal.

LIGHT VEGETARIAN LUNCH

- *Button Mushrooms in Oyster Sauce (page 96)*
- *Thai Aromatic Fried Rice (page 163)*
- *Green salad**
- *Fresh fruit**

Vegetables are a perfect solution for a light lunch. The mushrooms in a savoury oyster sauce are served with a very aromatic and satisfying Thai-flavoured fried rice dish and simple green salad. Fresh fruit is always the best solution for a light lunch dessert. The mushroom dish can be made in advance and reheats well.

COSY AUTUMN SUPPER

- *Sesame-Dressed Spinach Salad (page 74)*
- *Savoury Beancurd Casserole (page 122)*
- *Long-Grain Rice (page 160)*
- *Sweet Wuntuns (page 178)* **with vanilla ice cream***

This simple but savoury menu is perfect for cool autumn evenings. It begins with a sparkling spinach salad which can be made in the morning. The substantial and savoury beancurd dish may also be prepared in advance: it reheats well and is perfect over steamed long-grain rice. After all these nutritious foods, I like to indulge in crispy Sweet Wuntuns, which can also be made ahead of time. Serve them with Western vanilla ice cream – the best of East and West!

* Recipe not given in this book

VEGETARIAN FAMILY MEAL

■ *Tangy Tomato Soup with Lemongrass* (*page 60*)
■ *Vegetarian Chow Mein* (*page 142*)
■ *Crispy Vegetable Stir-Fry* (*page 112*)
■ *Malaysian Coconut Custard* (*page 179*)

This inspired menu could easily persuade your family to adopt the vegetarian style every day. The soup is a zesty and refreshing opener. Chow mein, of course, has a universal appeal and is a welcome addition to any meal. It is accompanied by the crunchy textured vegetable stir-fry, and finally there is a flavoured custard that is sure to please everyone. It can be served hot or cold. In this meal, as with most thoughtfully prepared vegetarian menus, your guests may never realise there is no meat, fish or poultry among the ingredients.

VEGETARIAN PARTY BUFFET

■ *Sugar Walnuts* (*page 41*)
■ *Crispy Vegetarian Wuntuns* (*page 49*)
■ *Japanese-Style Marinated Mushrooms* (*page 53*)
■ *Spicy Citrus-Flavoured Noodles* (*page 155*)
■ *Mock Vegetable Pasta* (*page 94*)
■ *Pineapple Fried Rice* (*page 166*)
■ *East–West Shredded Salad* (*page 75*)
■ *Assorted fresh fruit**

This is a delightful menu sure to please even non-vegetarians. Much of the work can be done beforehand. The Sugar Walnuts can be made up to 2 days in advance. Both the mushroom and noodle dishes can be made the night before. The Mock Vegetable Pasta can be made the morning of the buffet and will keep for hours in the refrigerator. Although the Pineapple Fried Rice is usually eaten hot, I find the sweet tartness of the pineapple equally appealing at room temperature. The salad is simple to make, and once the ingredients are prepared it takes but minutes to put it together. The wuntuns should ideally be fried just before serving. I would serve fresh fruit as the most appropriate dessert.

* Recipe not given in this book

ORIENTAL-STYLE PICNIC

- **Cold Sichuan Noodles** *(page 158)*
- **Crunchy Radish Salad** *(page 53)*
- **Stir-Fried Spicy Carrots** *(page 108)*
- **Cold Honeydew Dessert Soup** *(page 174)*

Picnics are a great favourite of mine, and foods flavoured with oriental spices add an exotic touch. This picnic menu is easy to assemble as the dishes can be made the day or night before and allowed to cool thoroughly, before being properly wrapped for the next day. Although the spicy carrots are usually served hot, I find them equally delicious cold. The salad offers a calming contrast to the noodles and carrots, both of which contain strong spices. The cold sweet soup has just the right cooling touch and makes a grand finale to the picnic.

COCKTAIL PARTY

- **Hot and Spicy Walnuts** *(page 43)*
- **Crispy Beancurd Cubes with Peanut Dipping Sauce** *(page 126)*
- **Winter Vegetable Fritters** *(page 49)*
- **Grilled Mushrooms with Lemon Sauce** *(page 106)*
- **Vegetable Medley with Tomato-Garlic Sauce** *(page 98)*

Cocktail parties are especially fun when good food is served. The food must be manageable so your guests can easily pick it up with cocktail sticks or fingers. And it must be easy on the host or hostess, so time can be spent with the guests. Therefore, most of this menu can be prepared hours in advance and all of it is 'finger-food'. The walnuts can be made the day before and re-crisped in the oven before serving. The dipping sauce can be made the night before, but the beancurd should be fried at the last possible moment. The fritters can be prepared at least 1 hour in advance and kept warm in a low oven. The grilled mushrooms are served at room temperature with the sauce made well in advance. Use the colourful vegetable medley as the centrepiece of your party, and prepare it the night before if necessary. This menu allows you to relax and enjoy your party with just a few last-minute touches.

DINNER IN A HURRY FOR TWO OR MORE

▪ *Spinach and Egg-Ribbon Soup (page 65)*
▪ *Sesame Buckwheat Noodles (page 154)*
▪ *Stir-Fried Lettuce (page 103)*
▪ *Fresh fruit**

This is a quick, nutritious dinner for two or more: the portions can easily be increased. The soup is a light stock with spinach and egg ribbons. The buckwheat noodles are satisfying and can be served warm or cold. They can be made ahead of time and kept in the refrigerator, but bring them to room temperature before serving. The lettuce takes but minutes to prepare and stir-fry. Fresh fruit is a sensible and delicious way to finish off this speedy yet wholesome meal.

SUMMER BARBECUE

▪ *Fragrant Rice Noodle Salad (page 156)*
▪ *Grilled Beancurd Shish Kebabs (page 116)*
▪ *Grilled barbecue chicken**
▪ *Fresh fruit in season**

Warm weather is a perfect environment for outdoor eating and grilling on a barbecue. This menu uses the best combination for a relaxed, carefree and informal way of eating. The noodle salad can be made hours in advance, freeing you to concentrate on the grill outside. Grilled beancurd is a delicious way to enjoy this nutritious food and, when combined with chicken, it provides a substantial plate. If you choose, you can alternate small tomatoes, squares of peppers and onions with the beancurd to make beancurd and vegetable shish kebabs. Of course, summer is the best time for a large variety of fresh summer fruits, and they are a perfect ending to any barbecue.

* Recipe not given in this book

VEGETARIAN DINNER PARTY
Photograph opposite page 144

■ *Asparagus with Tangy Mustard Dressing (page 80)*
■ *Braised Chinese Mushrooms (page 110)*
■ *Fragrant Coconut Rice (page 167)*
■ *Bean Sprout Salad (page 78)*
■ *Sweet Ginger Custard (page 175)*

Dinner parties offer one of the best reasons to cook for friends. Begin your meal with the asparagus, an elegant starter that sets the tone for the entire dinner. Braised Chinese Mushrooms can be made ahead of time and reheats well – it is a dish often served at Chinese banquets. The coconut rice is a flavoursome departure from the usual. A refreshing note is provided by the salad, which prepares you for the dessert. Sweet Ginger Custard is an Eastern variation of the universally popular vanilla custard, and rounds off the meal nicely.

COLD WINTER FEAST

■ *Fiery Sichuan Soup (page 67)*
■ *Stir-fried pork with vegetables* or*
■ *Grilled lamb chops**
■ *Cold Green Bean Salad (page 78)*
■ *Indonesian Fried Bananas (page 177)*

Cold winter evenings make for hearty appetites. This is a feast for family or friends, and the portions can easily be doubled. It begins with a hot and sour version of a well known Chinese soup that is sure to warm body and soul. I would follow this with a stir-fry pork dish perhaps, grilled lamb chops or any other meat you prefer. The Cold Green Bean Salad offers the perfect light contrast to the meats. The fried bananas make a tempting finishing touch, one that goes well with a good port.

* Recipe not given in this book

MAIL-ORDER SUPPLIERS

There are now many Chinese, oriental and Asian grocers throughout the UK. Below is a list of some which offer a mail-order service
for ingredients and cooking equipment.

Cheong-Leen Supermarket
4–10 Tower Street
Cambridge Circus
London W2 9NR
01–836 5378/9

Wah Fung Chinese Supermarket
146 Camden High Street
London NW1 0NE
01–485 6156

Ken Lo's Kitchen
14 Eccleston Street
London SW1W 0NZ
01–730 7734

Matahari Impex (Far East) Ltd
11 & 12 Hogarth Place
Earl's Court
London SW5 0QT
01–370 1041

Unico Trading Ltd
283 Water Road
Alperton
Middlesex HAO 1HX
01–998 2248

Man's Cafe
30 Spring Street
Portsmouth
Hants PO1 4AA
0705 822504

The Delicatessen
164 Old Christchurch Road
Bournemouth
Dorset BH1 1NU
0202 295979

Kam Cheung Chinese Supermarket
28–30 Burleigh Street
Cambridge CB1 1DG
0223 316429

Jason's Oriental Shop
16 Milton Road
Cambridge CB4 1JY
0223 68735

Chinese Emporium (Trading) Ltd
17 New London Road
Chelmsford
Essex CM2 0NA
0245 355535

P.K.M. Chinese Co Ltd
5 Melton Street
Leicester LE1 3NA
0533 29656

Quality Foods Cash and Carry
Quality House
Edderthorpe Street (off Leeds Road)
Bradford BD3 9JX
0274 393328/663944

Hondo Trading Co Ltd
149–153 Duke Street
Liverpool L1 4JR
051–708 5409

INDEX

A

Apples 176
Arachide oil *see* groundnut oil
Asparagus
  with Chinese black mush-
      rooms 99
  with Japanese rice 168
  with tangy mustard dress-
      ing 80, 186
  stir-fried in black bean
      sauce 95
Aubergine 85
  creamy, and tomato soup
      70
  peppery 72
  salad, Chinese 77
  Sichuan fried 102
Aubergines with sesame
      sauce 51

B

Bamboo shoots 11, 93
Banana crisps 175
Bananas
  crisps 175
  Indonesian fried 177, 186
Beancurd (doufu, tofu) 12
  'cakes' 12
  Cantonese-style, with
      Chinese greens 123
  casserole, savoury 122
  coconut-stewed, and veg-
      etables 124
  cubes with peanut dipping
      sauce 126
  custard, in oyster sauce 127
  dishes 115–128
  fermented 12
  fermented chilli 12, 101
  fermented red 122
  home-style spicy 117
  and mushroom stir-fry 119
  pan-fried, with leeks 127
  pressed, seasoned 12

red-cooked 125
shish kebabs, grilled 116
soft (silken tofu) 12
  and spinach soup 59
squares, stuffed 120
sweet and sour 118
Beancurd custard in oyster
      sauce 127
Beans
  black 13, 95, 104
  Chinese long 78, 87, 101
Bean sprout salad 78, 186
Bean sprouts 85, 92
Bitter melon with black bean
      sauce 104
Black beans 13
  sauce 95, 104
Blanching 33
Bok choi (Chinese greens) 87
Braised Chinese mushrooms
      110, 186
Braising 35
Broccoli 75, 93
  Chinese 86
Button mushrooms in oyster
      sauce 96, 182

C

Cabbage, Chinese flowering
      87
Cantonese-style beancurd
      with Chinese greens
      123
Carrots, stir-fried spicy 108
Cauliflower 75
  soup, Indonesian 63
Chicken stock 56
Chillies 13
  dried red 13–14, 20
  fresh 13
  oil 19
  powder (cayenne pepper)
      14
  sauce 20

Chilli oil/dipping sauce 20
Chinese anise *see* star anise
Chinese aubergine salad 77
Chinese flowering cabbage
      (choi sam) 87
Chinese greens (bok choi,
      Chinese white
      cabbage, Chinese
      chard) 87, 123
Chinese leaves (Chinese or
      Peking cabbage) 87
Chinese long beans 87
Chinese pancakes 39, 40, 96
Chinese parsley (coriander) 15
Chinese rice porridge with
      condiments 165
Chinese toffee apples 176
Chinese white radish (mooli)
      53, 88
Chives, Chinese 87
Chopping board 29
Chopsticks 30
Chow mein, vegetarian 142,
      183
Cinnamon sticks and bark 14
Cleavers 29
Cloud ears 18
  in hoisin sauce 106
  stir-fried with mange-tout
      105
Coconut milk 14
Coconut-stewed beancurd
      and vegetables 124
Cold Chinese noodle salad
      with mushrooms 150
Cold curry-flavoured noodles
      153
Cold dishes 71–81
Cold green bean salad 78, 186
Cold honeydew dessert soup
      174, 184
Cold Sichuan noodles 158,
      184
Cooking techniques
  blanching 33

braising and red-braising 35
deep-frying 34
poaching 33
reheating foods 36
shallow-frying or pan-frying 35
slow simmering and steeping 35
steaming 35
stir-frying 33
Coriander (Chinese parsley) 15
Cornflour 15
Corn (maize) oil 19
Creamy aubergine and tomato soup 70
Crispy beancurd cubes with peanut dipping sauce 126
Crispy cabbage with sugar walnuts 42
Crispy Cantonese-style noodles with vegetables 138
Crispy noodle salad 81
Crispy spring onion omelette 109
Crispy vegetable stir-fry 112, 183
Crispy vegetarian wuntuns 49, 183
Crunchy radish salad 53, 184
Cucumber
 hot and sour salad 73
 noodle salad 151
 stir-fried 107
Cucumber noodle salad 151
Curried fried rice with green beans 170
Curry paste 21
Cutting techniques 31–32
 diagonal slicing 32
 dicing 32
 horizontal or flat slicing 32
 roll cutting 32
 scoring 32
 shredding 32
 slicing 31

D
Dashi 16, 65, 100, 154

Deep-fat fryers 29, 34
Deep-frying 34
Desserts 173–180
Dipping sauces 22
Doufu (beancurd) 12
Dried lily buds see lily buds
Dry-braised bamboo shoots with broccoli 93

E
East–West shredded salad 75, 183
Eggs with Chinese mushrooms 111
Equipment 27–30

F
Fiery Sichuan soup 67
Fish sauce 22
Five spice powder 16
Fragrant coconut rice 167, 186
Fragrant noodle soup 68
Fragrant rice noodle salad 156, 185
Fresh pasta with coriander, ginger and basil pesto 133
Fried seaweed see crispy cabbage with sugar walnuts
Fun rice noodles 131, 146, 148
Fungus see mushrooms

G
Garlic 16
Ginger
 juice 17
 root 17
Golden needles see lily buds
Green beans in pungent sauce 101
Green and white jade salad 75
Grilled beancurd shish kebabs 116, 185
Grilled mushrooms with lemon sauce 106, 184
Groundnut (peanut) oil 19

H
Hoisin sauce 22
Home-made Chinese fresh rice 'fun' noodles 146
Home-made Chinese rice 'fun' noodles with peppers 148
Home-style spicy beancurd 117
Hong Kong-style fried rice 164
Hot and sour cucumber salad 73
Hot and sour noodles 140
Hot and spicy walnuts 43, 184

I
Indonesian cauliflower soup 63
Indonesian fried bananas 177, 186
Ingredients 11–26

J
Japanese rice with asparagus 168
Japanese seaweed soup 62
Japanese-style marinated mushrooms 53, 183

K
Korean bean thread sesame noodles with vegetables 136

L
Lemongrass 17
 tangy tomato soup with 60
Light and easy rice noodles 143
Lily buds (lily stems, golden needles) 17, 96

M
Malaysian coconut custard 179, 183
Mange-tout 88, 105
Mee krob 81

Melon
bitter 86, 104
honeydew 174
Mock vegetable pasta 94, 183
Mooli (Chinese white radish)
53, 88
Mung beans 86
Mushrooms
button 96, 106, 119
Chinese dried 17–18, 99,
110, 111, 169
cloud ears (black fungus)
18, 105, 106, 111
wood ears 18, 96
Japanese-style marinated
53
Mu-Shu vegetables with
Chinese pancakes 96

N
Noodles
bean thread 59, 132, 151
Korean, sesame, with
vegetables 136
spicy, with dried shrimps
134
buckwheat (soba) 131
sesame 154
Cantonese-style, with vegetables 138
egg 68, 130, 140, 145,
150, 153, 155, 157,
158
'fun' 131, 146, 148
rice 131, 143, 144, 146,
152
salad, fragrant 156
Singapore-style 141
with spinach 135
Tan Tan 139
Udon 131
in broth 137
Nori *see* seaweed
Northern Chinese vegetable
potstickers 46

O
Oils 18–19
Omelette, crispy spring onion
109
Oyster sauce 22

P
Pancakes
Chinese 39, 96
spring onion 40
Thai sweetcorn 38
Pan-fried beancurd with leeks
127
Pasta and noodles 8–9, 68,
81, 130
cold 149–158
hot 129–148
Peanuts 20
dipping sauce 46, 126
Peppers 90, 91, 92, 112, 148
Peppery aubergines 72
Pickled cabbage, Chinese 20,
25
red in snow 20, 42
spicy Korean kimchi 52
Pineapple fried rice 166, 183
Poaching 33
Potstickers, northern Chinese
vegetable 46

R
Radish, Chinese white (mooli)
53, 88
Rainbow vegetables in lettuce
cups 91
Red-cooked beancurd 125
Red in snow (Chinese pickled
cabbage) 20, 42
Reheating foods 36
Rice 159–171
cake 62
cookers 30
flour 16
glutinous 161, 162
flour 16, 181
long-grain 160
curried fried, with green
beans 170
fragrant coconut 167
Hong Kong-style fried
164
pineapple fried 166
Singapore lettuce fried
171
sweetcorn and ginger
fried 163
Thai aromatic fried 163
two-mushroom 169

paper wrappers 44
noodles 131
short-grain 161
Chinese porridge with
condiments 165
Japanese, with asparagus
168
steamed sticky 162
sizzling rice soup 61
vinegar 22
wine 20
Rice cake 62
Rice puffs with prune filling
180

S
Safflower oil 19
Sake 20
Salads 71–81
Sauces and pastes
black bean sauce 95, 104,
157
chilli bean sauce 21, 125
chilli sauce 21
curry paste 21
dipping sauces 22
fermented chilli beancurd
101
fish sauce 22
hoisin sauce 22, 106, 125
lemon sauce 106
oyster sauce 22, 96
peanut dipping sauce 46,
126
savoury sauce 120
sesame paste 22
sesame sauce 51
soy sauce 22
tomato-garlic sauce 98
yellow bean sauce 23
Savoury beancurd casserole
122, 182
Seaweed (nori) 23
fried *see* crispy cabbage with
sugar walnuts
soup, Japanese 62
Sesame
oil 19
paste 22
sauce, with aubergines 51
seeds 23
toasted 23

Sesame buckwheat noodles 154, 185
Sesame-dressed spinach salad 74, 182
Shallots 88
Shallow-frying 35
Sherry, as substitute for rice wine 24
Shrimps, dried 24, 134
Sichuan
  fiery soup 67
  peppercorns 20, 24
    in five spice powder 16
    roasted 24, 73, 125
  preserved vegetable 24, 139, 162
Simple beancurd and mushroom stir-fry 119
Singapore noodles 145
Singapore-style lettuce fried rice 171
Singapore-style rice noodles 141
Sizzling rice soup 61
Slow simmering 35
Soft beancurd and spinach soup 59
Soups 55–70
Southeast Asian noodle salad 152
Southeast Asian vegetable soup 69
Soya bean oil 19
Soy sauces 22–23
Spicy bean thread noodles with dried shrimps 134
Spicy black bean sauce noodles 157
Spicy citrus-flavoured noodles 155, 183
Spicy Korean kimchi 52
Spicy peanut sauce 46
  with spring rolls 44
Spinach
  Chinese water 89
  and egg-ribbon soup 65, 185
  in oyster sauce 76
  and rice noodles 135
  salad, sesame-dressed 74
Spinach and egg-ribbon soup 65, 185

Spinach in oyster sauce 76
Spinach and rice noodles 135
Spring onion omelette, crispy 108
Spring onion pancakes 40
Spring rolls 44
Star anise 25, 42
  in five spice powder 16
Starters and appetisers 37–54
Steamed sticky rice 162
Steamed vegetable soup 66
Steamers 30
Steaming 35
Stir-fried asparagus in black bean sauce 95
Stir-fried cucumbers 107
Stir-fried 'silver sprouts' 92
Stir-fried spicy carrots 108, 184
Stir-fried vegetables over a rice noodle cloud 144
Stir-frying 33
Stock 56, 58
Stuffed beancurd squares 120
Sugar 25
Sugar walnuts 41, 183
Summer pepper stir-fry 90
Sunflower oil 19
Sweetcorn
  and ginger custard 175, 186
  and ginger fried rice 163
  and ginger soup 64
  pancakes, Thai 38
Sweet and sour beancurd 118
Sweet wuntuns 178, 182

T
Tangy tomato soup with lemongrass 60, 183
Tan Tan noodles 139
Thai aromatic fried rice 163, 182
Thai sweetcorn pancakes 38
Tiger lily buds see lily buds
Tofu (beancurd) 12

U
Udon noodles in broth 137

V
Vegetable dishes 83–113

Vegetable medley with tomato-garlic sauce 98, 184
Vegetable pasta, mock 94
Vegetable soup, Southeast Asian 69
Vegetable stir-fry, crispy 112
Vegetable stock 58
Vegetable tempura 100
Vegetables, Vietnamese-style 113
Vegetarian chow mein 142, 183
Vietnamese-style vegetables 113
Vietnamese-style vegetarian spring rolls 44
Vinegars 25–26
  black rice 22, 26
  cider 25
  malt 25
  red rice 22, 26
  white rice 26

W
Walnuts
  crispy cabbage with sugar 42
  hot and spicy 43
  sugar 41, 183
Waterchestnuts 89
Whole anise see star anise
Winter vegetable fritters 49, 184
Wok 27–28
  accessories 28–29
  Cantonese and pau 27
Wuntuns, crispy vegetarian 49, 183
Wuntun skins 26

Y
Yellow bean sauce 23, 93, 117, 144, 148, 157, 158